SELF-WORTH IS ONLY ACHIEVED THROUGH SPORTS

A REFRESHING, HIGH-OCTANE ROMP ACROSS THE LANDSCAPE OF OUR FAVORITE PASTIMES WITH THE EDITOR OF OREGON SPORTS NEWS...WITH WHOM WE ALMOST GOT ARRESTED

PATRICK MCNERTHNEY

CONTENTS

For Rowyn

FOREWORD

BY ARRAN GIMBA

FALL 2021

For those who don't know me (and that would be 99.9% of you…hi, Mom!), my name is Arran Gimba and I am the founder and editor-in-chief of Oregon Sports News (oregonsportsnews.com). Oregon Sports News is a local sports commentary site that has been around since 2011. We've had an amazing group of writers come and go, with many ending up becoming household names.

And then there's Patrick McNerthney.

Patrick McNerthney is, without a shadow of doubt, the most creative writer I've ever had (Patrick, you know my Venmo, you can pay me now). He's like if Tony Kornheiser, Larry David, and Bill Simmons had a baby (which, scientifically, not sure how that is possible but it's a fun trope). His writing doesn't fit into any of the preselected categories on Oregon Sports News. Not a Seattle Seahawks writer, not Portland Trail Blazers, sort of/kind of health and fitness but not really. I told him at one point I should just dedicate a category to him (which I haven't because that takes, you know, effort).

When I get a column from Patrick, I have no idea what to expect. I know this is mostly my fault because I never give my team topics that they must write about. I'm one of those creative, artistic freedom kind of hippies. From cheer-leading to fishing to bear crawls to sportsbooks to hunting to looking good at the gym, you tell me what category makes the most sense.

But you know what? I love it (Venmo reminder, Patrick). It gives the site so much more depth. It's more than just talking about how the Seattle Mariners will fail its fans this season (hint: they will fail…and it will be spectacular). He really provides us with a fresh perspective that, seriously, you can't get anywhere else.

As you read his columns in this book, you'll understand why I get a smile every time I read his work for reviewing and posting. The smile is really one of self-gratification over how much time Grammarly saves me on editing. BUT I'm sure part of it is also about Patrick.

Enjoy!

GETTING IN SHAPE IS NOT A TEAM SPORT

WINTER 2021

The Super Bowl is over, and the other team won.

I'm fairly certain this is how 95% of the country views the outcome of this painful event. That and the fact that the advertising seemed a bit lackluster. Usually someone at least does an ad with monkeys — did that happen? Was I too busy stuffing my face with barbecue to notice? And trying to endear myself to the hosts by looking like I was helping with the dishes in hopes of an invitation to return next year — when surely someone besides the Unmentionable Perfect Robot Quarterback will be playing — so I missed my beloved orangutan-themed ad?

Well, monkeys or no, it's over, but don't fret, there's lots of other sports stuff to look forward to. February is ripe with sweaty happenings designed for the sports lover, as it features lots of...ah...golf. There's quite a bit of golf in February, I think. Oh, there's also NASCAR and other Ludicrous Speed Racing Events involving various kinds of vehicles that tend to explode. That's always good for a few minutes (albeit impossible to watch in its entirety; I think a race takes five business days to complete).

Then there's the *Sports Illustrated* swimsuit issue (literally created to fill the post—Super Bowl sports void, not that I'm admitting there's any kind of void here and further offending those I'm already offending), and I think tennis is happening. Yes, tennis! Check out the all the beautifully genteel folks at the BNP Paribas Open and think about what a sweet, classy, clean sport tennis is — it just screams Sergio Tacchini sweatsuits, rolls of cash, and chilling out on the French Riviera. And possibly overly bronzed bankers.

Wait! There's also spring training for Major League Baseball. That's where the players go to warm climates to get tan and occasionally get in trouble at strip clubs while the rest of us freeze. Not unlike the perpetuity of auto racing, there are, I think, 872 games in the Cactus League before the real 1,756-game season kicks off April 1st.

Oh yeah, there's basketball too, college and otherwise, plus a few other sports I can't remember, like hockey.

So basically you're screwed as far as sports fandom is concerned, and it's time I took off the gloves and really drove the point home because you're in denial and I'm the best friend… and speaking of best friends, I need to borrow 150 bucks.

This lull in the sports season that everyone (except straight-shooting best friend here, who always has your back) refuses to admit is a lull is the perfect time to maybe dial back on the beer a bit and get back into fighting shape. There's lots to look forward to this spring, so might as well look your best. Besides, what if there's a fight? Can't just jump out in the street and start punching without training first — you'll just get flipped upside down on the front lawn in front of the family, and the whole neighborhood will point and laugh at you. Trust me on this one.

Since you're probably wondering how on earth you're going to do this, I decided to create a brief yet extraordinarily helpful exercise guide to examine and later pay me for. So put down the cinnamon roll and start thinking about which of the following very aptly described physical fitness routines to select and thus make your world a better place:

Peloton — This is a great subscription-based app filled with beautiful fitness models who offer encouraging mantras to hyperventilate to regardless of the selected workout. No need to buy the

$5,000.00 bike for cycling routines, although Peloton would appreciate it.

Muddy Hill near House — Nothing says "impressive" more than a middle-aged person toughening themselves up by sprinting up the muddy hill behind their house rain or shine, then doing 20 push-ups every time they reach the summit. Think CrossFit with way more street cred. Caution: Only insane people do this. Like my very fit neighbor, who obviously has something to prove.

CrossFit — This is a club mostly consisting of people who never played sports in high school and want to show up their classmates who did play sports at the next reunion. There's actually a physician on staff to write an immediate referral for chiropractic and physical therapy services after each session.

Weight Lifting — You can sort of go to a gym now, and gyms tend to have lots of weights, so that would probably be good for your mental health, even if it's just getting you out of the house for a minute. Speaking of which, if you didn't buy weights for your house back in March when everything shut down, they're all gone, so don't even bother going to Big 5 or Walmart or whatever. More will be available in 2023.

Yoga — On the surface this seems like it would be really easy, but it's definitely not. There are plenty of yoga apps out there, but it's hard to find one where you don't end up just looking at pornography. Bikram is a popular form of yoga that incorporates a 105° temperature with steam

(40% humidity) — the best way to make this happen given social isolation is to run the shower for an hour and do the poses on the toilet.

Cycling — Heralded as the sport of dorks, cycling is actually really fun and liberating as long as you don't succumb to fashion. Oh, you need to be extremely wealthy to cycle, so if that's not your deal, please move on.

Running — A.k.a. "laterally grimacing," this one certainly possesses the lowest entry barrier of all these workouts since all you need are shoes, some form of pathway, and a violent-crime-free neighborhood. Please note there's a reason why people who run carry an expression of resigned discomfort and often have tape covering every joint below their elbows.

That's it. There are no other options; choose one of the above.

The most important thing to take away from all this madness is that you've really let yourself go the past few months and it's inexcusable. It doesn't matter that it's winter and miserable out, or that life now consists of the four walls of the house and your entire family on top of you and driving you nuts. The good sports to watch are over, might as well take all of your newfound spare time and do something productive with it — like whipping yourself into shape. Think of the impact it will make on your mental and physical health. It's going to be great.

Also, if you follow any of the above recommended workout routines there's a waiver at the bottom of this page you have to sign, date, notarize, and return. To me, in an envelope, with 150 bucks.

YOU DON'T HAVE WHAT IT TAKES TO TEACH PHYSICAL EDUCATION

WINTER 2021

I ran into an old acquaintance the other day — he teaches health and fitness at a local high school. This is what physical education (P.E.) is called in modern times, as far as I can tell. In my day it was called "Teacher's Assistant Who Plays Football and Is an Idiot Hits Freshmen with Pickleball Paddle."

After speaking with him (my acquaintance, not the idiot), I grew quite unsettled by the notion of working in a field entirely based on doing one's best to create positive change for people, as this is apparently what modern-day teachers do. Hey teachers, where's your greed, self-interest, and unending quest for newer/better material things? Come on now.

To make matters worse, a sports podcaster I follow (I will not refer you to his podcast until he pays me royalties or at least returns my calls or lifts the restraining order) recently made a statement about leadership that made me quite upset. This buffoon stated, "Leadership is making sure the people you are responsible for are always taken care of."

What? What about leading with fear and intimidation to enforce your status like the aforementioned P.E. Teacher's Assistant, who with my luck got on early at Netflix and is now worth ten million dollars?

And what about the leadership I grew up with? You know, culling the weak and creating distrust/paranoia by pitting people against each other, thereby further cementing positions of authority? Like they do in the Chinese Communist Party — or possibly in the United States Senate. Oh, and the office of the NBA Commissioner. I heard that place can be rough.

I'm sorry, but do you think Patrick Mahomes, the de facto leader of the Kansas City Chiefs just like all quarterbacks are de facto leaders of their teams much to the chagrin of the long snapper and to a lesser degree an offensive guard, wants to make sure his fellow teammates are "always taken care of"? No way, he…well, I mean, I don't know him actually. On the surface he appears kind of nice, like you could invite him over for dinner and he'd come and bring a really good dessert and have impressive table manners.

And then there is that notion of offensive linemen "taking care of" the quarterback. As in, they have his back no matter what. And the Chiefs are playing on Sunday, which is kind of a big deal, so something is working for them in terms of this completely-counterintuitive-to-the-notion-of-capitalism-and-rugged-American-individualism style of leadership.

Okay, fine, perhaps leadership *can* be about taking care of those you're responsible for. So this begs the question: Who in their right mind would do that? My acquaintance, apparently… through teaching physical education…ah…health and fitness, that is.

Get this. Health and fitness teachers (and I imagine it applies to all academic subjects and extracurriculars, including band, sports, clubs, plays, musicals, etc.) basically have multiple altruistic goals that focus on meeting each student *where they're at* rather than just cramming a blanket curriculum down their throat. Or hitting them with a pickleball paddle.

For example, health and fitness teachers accommodate all spectrums of ability, so if it's volleyball day they adjust the activities so the varsity death-spiker kids get as much exercise as the kids who can't even throw the ball to themselves. This is apparently called "differentiation." I wish I had been differentiated in high school. I'm not kidding. I would be saving thousands on psychotherapy — or, as my wife calls it, "crazy whispering."

Then, even though there are boxes to check to meet required national standards/curriculums, the priority for health and fitness teachers is to organize activities, games, and drills that develop healthier lifestyles *and* get the kids moving. I envision them sitting in the teacher's lounge (or teacher's lounge Zoom call, given COVID-inspired hybrid learning/workplaces), saying, "Screw you, bureaucracy! Yeah, your box is checked, don't worry about it."

These health and fitness leaders want to get the kids moving because, even prior to the pandemic, the amount of time young people spend on physical education is in decline. It's just not emphasized as much as science, technology, engineering, and math (STEM)…which is tragic and, in my opinion, provides more fodder for making fun of technology and its nefarious aims in particular (i.e., right now you're likely thinking of your Instagram feed instead of this article, which is no accident, and highly offensive.)

I don't have a beef with science, math, or engineering, mostly because I like my bridges, buildings, etc. intact.

(Have you ever thought about how compulsory education was established in the early 20th century to create good workers for the growing manufacturing industry? Do you think that's happening now with the "T" from "STEM," to benefit the tech industry?)

And with the pandemic, these already slovenly messes (the kids) have gotten in worse shape.

According to my acquaintance, one-mile run times are up 15% over last year, and it's not infrequent to overhear a high schooler saying, "I was in so much better shape pre-COVID" while they're outside in the parking lot after school wrestling with each other and talking with their masks off.

Come on, don't act so surprised. We're talking ninth-graders here. They can't keep their hands off each other. And yes, I made up that 15% statistic, but it's true kids get less exercise as a result of technology, educational curriculums, and (now) COVID. Go ahead, do the Google. I bet those run times are up really close to 15%.

So health and fitness teachers recognize the importance of movement as a tool to build self-esteem in these soft monsters. But how does one do this virtually? With half the class in-person and half the class on Zoom, how do you coordinate activities where everyone will participate while dealing with the age-old problem of varying levels of fitness, not to mention these kids' insecurities, peer pressure, raging hormones, and all that other teenage stuff?

Think online workouts à la Peloton.

Would you have thought of that? I doubt it.

Why is this brilliant? Because everyone's attention is on the video and *not on each other*. I wish I'd had a way to distract people from witnessing my wheezing, uncoordinated attempts at exercise in high school. Wait, I wish I had that now.

But those crafty teachers don't stop there. They continue to adapt to virtual fitness education by creating activities like these:

Every Minute on the Minute (EMOM) — Twenty minutes of exercise broken down by the minute with cameras ON; if you finish early (e.g., after 40 seconds), you get 20 seconds of rest. (I tried this and almost died.)

Time Lapse — Do whatever you want (go for a walk, do push-ups, etc.), but use your phone to take a time-lapse video the entire time and turn it in. (I tried this and almost got arrested because I'm an adult and it thus looks suspicious.)

Would You Rather? — Your answer determines your workout; i.e., would you rather eat a burger or an ice cream, then here's the workout that burns that amount of calories. (I answered honestly with "both" and thus had to run a half marathon.)

Break Out — Form small groups with a student leader (the teacher is deliberately absent to place the onus on the kids), pick a workout, record it as a group, then turn it in. (I tried to get my friends to do this and they told me, quite vehemently, there was no way they'd agree to it.)

These adaptations all have the same goal: get kids moving by challenging each student at their individual level, providing independence, and giving them something to focus on besides each other.

Turns out those teachers are a cunning bunch, right? I'd argue that caring for their students while adapting to a hyper-fluid environment like COVID is possibly going above their pay grade. (As previously stated, I'm dumbfounded by anything that isn't designed to fill up coffers with gold. And I'm still struggling to understand this concept of generous, empathetic leadership.)

So do you think you could hack it as a P.E. instructor for ninth-graders, especially during COVID? I don't care if you're an investment banker, firefighter, or (dreaded) C-level executive at a technology company; I think the answer is no.

Maybe Patrick Mahomes could do it, though.

SELF-WORTH IS ONLY
ACHIEVED THROUGH VICTORY

Pickleball may be one of the greatest sports ever invented. If you've never played, think miniature tennis with wooden rackets, a plastic ball, a shorter court, a lower net…okay, this doesn't sound like tennis at all; think giant ping-pong. But less nerdy as there's actually enough physical movement to get winded and sweat profusely.

Speaking of which, ping-pong is also a pretty groovy sport, especially in the winter as it provides an opportunity for concentrated power of will and skill while drinking beer indoors with heat and light. But watch out, ping-pong tends to bring out the worst in people, especially the owner of the table, who's undoubtedly logged more (recent) playing time, so even though you have pretty good hand-eye coordination, prepare to get absolutely smoked by this fool, who during play will avidly communicate how badly you're getting smoked, since you're getting smoked. In his big fancy house. Which you resent. Obviously.

This is why I made a drastic change midcareer and left the drunken, broken-paddled world of Nobody Cares, Amateur Ping-Pong at My Friend's House and entered the American National Pickleball Circuit of America (ANPCA) as the number one unranked amateur of 1993.

This little-known circuit spans the states of Washington, Oregon, Ohio, New York, and to a lesser degree Arkansas. It's the precursor to the now extremely popular and scandal-laden Pro Pickleball Association (PPA), United States of America Pickleball Association (USAPA), and Sexaholics Anonymous.

Just as modern-day NFL players look back in awe at the lunatics who ran into goalposts with leather helmets in the 1940s, modern-day pickleball players (upon learning I was in ANPCA in the '90s) often stop me at strip malls and ask for my autograph, then insist I have a bite of their sandwich. Which I decline (the bite, not the autograph), as I have class.

This respect exists because today's pros (whom we founders find soft, spoiled, and generally ripe with overscented deodorant — we used Pine-Sol in our pits in the '90s) know some of the best athletes in the world participated in the ANPCA at one time or another, typically at the beginning of their careers, including boxer Floyd Mayweather and NFL great John Elway. I can tell you a humdinger of a story about playing doubles with Floyd Mayweather, but I'll save that for another time.

I entered the pro circuit at the age of 19, and contrary to modern professional sports protocols that encourage training and specialization starting at about age 6, I was considered quite the phenom as pickleball requires a level of maturity and mental sharpness typically found in 27-year-old postdoctoral students at Emory University. What can I say? I had it together upstairs.

And the rest of me…well, my footwork was "impeccable," according to Tony Roche, I already told you about my hand-eye coordination (were you listening?), and my paddle head speed generated a new form of spin on the wiffle…ah, pickleball itself, which came to be known as "lots of pickling."

Training consisted of working with various coaches we'd meet on tour, many of whom lacked credentials and were simply neighborhood eccentrics, but they nonetheless pushed us Professional Pickleballers to an athletic level typically reserved for highly profitable yet unpaid Division I football players or disc golf enthusiasts. Days began at 6:00 a.m. sharp in the weight room, our workouts focusing entirely on bicep curls and neck extensions. Then we'd hit serves for an hour outside no matter the weather (back then the ANPCA lacked any indoor facilities; we veterans scoff at the kids these days playing indoors, what with their forced-air heating/cooling and practical athletic shoes that offer comfort, support, and style…they probably wear lacy gloves too…I think hitting pickleballs in the snow made me the champion I was and a better father and husband today.)

Unfortunately the rest of life on the circuit was pretty rough. With no large corporate sponsors (my understanding is the league was financed entirely by regional banks that found themselves in desperate circumstances, with additional funding provided by the trainers' proclivity for placing winning "show" bets at the track), no private jets were available so we in the league were forced to attend tournaments via Amtrak or, in really bad years, Greyhound buses. Naturally, being forced to take slow, American public transportation led to large outbreaks of sexually transmitted diseases and rampant drug abuse, including tobacco, Valium, and malt liquor. Typically all at once.

I remember being so confused after a 37-hour bus ride to Akron that I actually went on Center Court and played my guitar until the sobbing tournament organizers were able to convince the Head Landscaper to use his pressure washer to crowd-control me off the premises.

Most of us were able to pull it together, though, thanks to the help of our fellow circuit member Lorenzo Giustino, a disgraced psychotherapist who joined the league as part of his sentencing requirement. Lorenzo got us off the substance abuse and sex addiction through a series of cognitive exercises that focused on creating self-worth only through our ability (or lack thereof) to win the 1993 U.S. Open Pickleball Championship in Brockport, New York.

Many people ask me about my magnum opus. Was it creating a Fortune 500 company? The birth of my son? Can childbirth be a magnum opus? What does the term actually mean? No, my magnum was that 1993 U.S. Open Pickleball Championship in Brockport. Which is a nice town you should visit; bring the family and everything.

By this time I was a household name as far as pickleball fans were concerned. As I swaggered onto the court, fresh off drugs and high on life, I grew concerned the grandstand would collapse due to the throngs of topless fans, most of whom unfortunately were truck drivers, jumping up and down with undulating bellies, screaming my name, eating gas station microwave burritos, and throwing back delicious beer after beer I so desperately wanted. I remember thinking, "No, keep your beer to yourselves, you cornerstones of our nation's commercial infrastructure, this premier athlete only drinks adrenaline and an occasional Bartles and Jaymes wine cooler. Don't tell Lorenzo."

For the first time in my career, my opponent was from outside the ANPCA, a clever Serbian by the name of Milica Johnson. "Johnson?" I asked him. "Milica *Johnson*? What kind of a Serbian name is that?" Which was a huge mistake as my standard effort to conduct psychological warfare by making fun of things people have no control over back-fired when he replied that he was going to kill me. I was so scared.

The 1993 U.S. Open Pickleball Championship lasted a grueling 4.5 hours — still a record to this day. (Most matches take about 22 minutes, which is why pickleball is a favorite among those suffering from short attention spans. Or sex addiction.) I still have on my living room wall photos snapped by paparazzi of my rugged, glis-tening, stripped-to-the-waist form, much to the chagrin of our houseguests (which are somehow rare) — that's how hot it was on the court…in fact, to this day June 21st, 1993, is the hottest day every recorded in Brockport.

Milica and I battled it out to the last second. He'll claim he won based on skill, his incredible ability to focus thanks to having a father who pioneered modern sports psychology (whom Pete Carroll studied under at one point, or so I hear), and the overall score. But I know he won thanks to some shady calls and the fact that my pickleball racket had a teeny splinter coming out of the bottom of the handle that affected my pickling ability.

But it's still my magnum opus. At the awards ceremony I made sure to bombard Milica with bois-terous, hilarious, and profane catcalls because I'm a terrible sport and I hated him for winning. Eventually I was chased off by that pressure-washer-wielding landscaper. I have no idea how he found me.

If you've never tried it, you should give it a go. Pickleball is a sport of the ages, designed for all ages, and can lead to great things, as I have duly attested. Besides, realistically, do you have anything better to do right now?

NATIONAL FORESTS NEED MORE READILY AVAILABLE PARKING

WINTER 2021

I know a guy who likes to bowhunt. I can tell because spanning the entire width of the rear window of his humongous Ford F-350 is a decal that says "Bowhunter," above an image of a similarly humongous arrow, complete with a deadly-looking broadhead (the pointy part that kills things), fletchings (which were the feathers on the backs of arrows in days of old but are now parabolic-shaped plastics designed to guide the missile to its target), and a nock (the de facto firing pin of an arrow, i.e., a notch that engages the bowstring for launching).

As you can likely surmise, I myself am not a bowhunter and in fact prefer to stay nice and cozy inside warm, insulated structures, preferably with some form of bar or cocktail lounge available. That being said, I enjoy hunting birds with modern firearms, meaning shotguns, which requires lots of effort but overall not nearly the effort and patience it takes to bowhunt.

Or hunt wild boar. My Texan cousins took my brother-in-law wild boar hunting once. It involved driving to the middle of 1,000 acres of mixed farm/scrub land with two gigantic Dobermans, complete with spiked collars. At night. Then the four of them plus two dogs started walking through the midnight fields until the Dobermans/Cerberuses caught wind of a wild boar, which led them on a two-hour chase featuring several fence-hoppings (and therefore trespassings) until they cornered the angry, crop-ruining bacon depository in a gully and the dogs grabbed ahold of it. At which point my cousins handed my brother-in-law a large Crocodile Dundee–styled knife, which he asked what to do with, as anyone working in the professional services industry is wont to do when handed a gigantic blade in the humid dark of south-central Texas. The answer was to bury it in the boar's neck. Which he did. I still think he goes to therapy over the whole thing, much to my cousins' delight.

I've never been to Texas.

The bowhunting thing is essentially the same process minus the mythological dog references and knife-wielding mayhem. You basically head up to the mountains (at least in Washington State), dress head-to-toe in camouflage, dump a bunch of human-scent-blocking juice all over your gear and flesh (those deer and elk have good sniffers), climb a tree, stand precariously on said tree hopefully with the aid of a tree stand (platform), and wait for the beast to walk under your tree so you can bury an arrow in its neck or heart or lung.

My understanding is that most effective shots happen at 20 yards or less, although I've only ever heard one bowhunter admit this — most spin yarns detailing 60-yard shots between trees in the face of howling maelstroms while somehow simultaneously fixing the kitchen sink.

Of course, once the animal is deceased, you have to field dress (gut) it and pack it out to God knows where you parked. The United States Forest Service (USFS) should install more readily available parking in our national forests, like right at the top of various mountains. They could make a killing off the hourly fees, although I imagine it would be hard for the attendants to hop from mountain to mountain to chalk people's tires and give out exorbitantly large fines for exceeding hourly limits. Anyway, well-located parking lots, or even large garages, would make the pack-out easier for hunters — have you seen how big an elk is?

Once you've brought the animal back to your vehicle, which is likely located at least partially near a fairly well-traveled state or federal road system, you have to load it up while hoping no activist-minded city folk drive by and tell you what a horrible person you are. In a way I understand their shock — I recently drove back from a bird hunting trip and saw two guys struggling to lift a slightly bloodied blacktail deer into the back of their pickup truck. The legs kind of flopped around in a disturbing manner, so I can see how schlepping around dead animals can appear undignified or disrespectful — but then again most modern civilians probably don't really understand what harvesting animals is like on a farm or anywhere else.

(In 1986 I took my Washington State Hunter's Safety course. They were big on educating hunters to respect the animal, the land, property owners, and certainly the public, encouraging the latter by discouraging the old hunter habits of tying deceased deer to the roof, trunk, or even hood of their vehicle for the voyage home…or stringing game birds across the bumper.)

Once you're back in your vehicle, it's important to remember to take off all your weird gear — you don't want to stop for gas or a snack dressed like a QAnon supporter or other form of military anarchist. It's just not good for the public's mental health or, really, our democracy.

At this point you ultimately have to decide whether you're going to butcher the deer or elk yourself or take it to a professional. My buddy Joe lives on a farm and does all his own butchering, which makes sense (he makes really good jalapeño venison sticks). Speaking of which, your murderous spree generates all kinds of delectable treats — venison or elk steaks, jerky, sausage, ground beef…well, it's not beef but you get the idea…and probably other stuff I don't know about that's really quite delicious.

All in all you can see where my preference for shooting a pheasant, putting it in the special dead bird compartment of my hunting vest, cleaning it, then retiring to a motel preferably located close to a Mexican restaurant comes from. What can I say, I like ease of use and margaritas. And pheasant, which tastes like exotic chicken. This bowhunting business (or really just hunting fairly gigantic four-legged animals with anything) is way above my pay grade.

My son recently asked for and received a recurve bow. This is a bow with limbs that curve away from the archer when unstrung; once it's strung, the resulting tension stores more energy and delivers energy more efficiently than a straight-limbed bow. So far I've (a) assembled it incorrectly several times and (b) spent an inordinate amount of time figuring out how to actually get the bowstring on, almost injuring myself in the process. At least it's not a compound bow (using a levering system consisting of cables and pulleys — very powerful, weapon of choice for bowhunters), which would take me a year to figure out. But it does seem like he's very interested in bowhunting, given that he keeps talking about broadheads and dead deer despite my attempts to change the subject. And he really does love going to this walk-through archery range that has animal bag targets in a natural hunting setting.

Frankly, I'm just glad to get him outside.

Sounds like I'll need to get in better shape. And call the USFS to tell them about my parking idea.

FAST FOOD AND NCAA-SPONSORED GAMBLING

WINTER 2021

'Tis the season when moderately avid sports fans suddenly realize semiprofessional to professional unpaid NCAA college athletes have been playing basketball since sometime in November. Rabid fans, players, coaches, family members, groupies, and gambling addicts have, of course, been aware of this fact all along and are paying rapt attention to various outcomes, sometimes resulting in visits to various boat or possibly yacht sales floors.

Or, unfortunately, a call from a bookie.

That's right, it's March, a long month (there's actually 34 days and I can tell you where they're hidden if you pay me) devoid of holidays created by advertising agencies (St. Patrick's Day being technically invented by religion in an attempt to gain access to eternal life), frequented by

still-terrible weather (although places other
than the Pacific Northwest and Alaska start to
see glimmers of spring), and ripe with growing
fears of having to do our taxes (I don't pay
taxes — don't tell anyone), made slightly more
palatable by the opportunity to drink Shamrock
Shakes (we just meant advertising agencies didn't
invent St. Patrick's Day; we never claimed multinational corporations haven't figured out ways to
profit from it).

I, for one, do enjoy me a Shamrock Shake, way
more than the McRib.

So, with March comes the madness. Er, Madness® —
at least I think it's a registered trademark, I
don't want to get in trouble here. The NCAA is
terrifying, and I assume they're omniscient,
incredibly buff Evil Genius Supervillains. How
else can you explain their convincing a bunch of
premier athletes to make various schools tons of
money and then not give them a cut? Anyway, I
like to call the NCAA Division I Men's Basketball
Tournament the "Age of Madness."

(For the record, any Division II or III Championship Tournament, as well as the much less
commercially lauded NCAA Division I Women's
Basketball Tournament — and really any college
sport, men's or women's, where young athletes
compete while adults froth at the mouth over the
potential for personal gain — can be categorized
as a part of the Age of Madness).

As previously implied, the defining character-
istic of this Age is gambling, specifically at

work, which is technically illegal and certainly unreasonable and possibly dangerous if you're operating heavy equipment. But again, we're not calling it Madness for nothing.

My first foray into the world of office betting pools — ah, perhaps we should call them company-sanctioned competitions only accessible during lunch breaks, so we don't get in trouble — was in 1995, when I played Fantasy Football for the first time. Back then, most of you were likely not alive, which makes me upset, but it's impor-tant for you to understand how analog it was. I worked a summer job in an over-air-conditioned office filled with '90s business casual wearers (think pleated khakis and short-sleeve button-up shirts). The Draft (back then it was just called "the draft") happened over the course of one hour, utilizing a conference table, legal pads, pens, and stats from the sports page of the local paper, along with several issues of *Sports Illustrated*.

Ha! Now *that's* research. You soft young people with your apps and streaming services and Draft Kings accounts and scrolling binary statistics. You don't know how easy you've got it. Your only hand cramps come from feverishly trying to keep your opinions atop a Fantasy Reddit thread as you desperately mash on your phone in some desperate attempt at creating self-worth.

Whoa, what happened there? Sorry about that. I'm having some rage issues of late. Let's keep this thing moving, shall we?

I recall using the first pick of the entire draft on a wide receiver by the name of J.J. Stokes (drafted by the 49ers…my healthy loathing of anything from the Bay Area hadn't fully developed yet). Next, I drafted a kicker. At this point, based on the expressions of the poorly dressed, middle-aged men who owned my employ — women really weren't invited to play Fantasy Football, which is terrible and sexist, and a typical yet completely illogical thing for a group of seemingly heterosexual males to do; it's like purposefully not inviting girls, or whoever you like, to your house party — I realized I had made a terrible mistake.

Thus, thanks to incompetence, I had an awful fantasy season and lost $100.00 in cold hard cash. Adjusted for inflation, this is like losing your house today.

The following year (that's 1996, for those not paying attention), this same group invited me to "fill out a bracket" ostensibly related to March Madness®…ah, the Age of Madness. So I steadfastly ignored my disastrous Fantasy Football season, filled out the stupid thing (with a pen), and upped the ante to $200.00. All without wondering why I was being invited back, given that I didn't work there anymore. Hmmmmm.

Of course, I also lost this wise investment. I blame it on a serious of cataclysmic gastrointestinal issues suffered by Wake Forest before their Sweet 16 game against Kentucky, which turned out to be not so sweet. Or maybe I just lost it because I'm not good at gambling. Or sports. Which is why I now officially scowl at the mention of Fantasy Football and/or the Age of Madness. Especially if they're somehow mentioned simultaneously. And especially if someone is paying attention to me, which is a rare event indeed.

Despite my distaste for these events, I have to admit that between the two, the Age of Madness is a bigger deal. In fact, I'd like to formerly stake the claim that the Age of Madness® is Officially Better Than Fantasy Football®. That second "®" is mine; I just registered the phrase with the U.S. Patent and Trademark Office, don't touch it.

I know you're tired and likely hankering for a bourbon and Squirt® — which is delicious if you haven't tried it but really more of a summertime thing so maybe you should wait until then, plus you have to be careful 'cause it goes down real smooth, which is why I like to call them Wobbly-pops — so let me enlighten you as to why Madness beats Fantasy. To expedite the process I'll henceforth refer to the championship tournament as March Madness.

First of all, the betting pools behind March Madness coined an entirely new word: bracketol-ogy. What "-ology" has Fantasy Football ever made? I guess it contributes to "psychology," considering the several nervous breakdowns I've witnessed when "garbage time" during a real-life NFL game determines the outcome of a tight fantasy game. Nervous breakdowns are so fun to watch when it's not you! But still, Fantasy Football? Officially Not As Good.

Next, the NCAA Tournament spreads joy throughout otherwise dreary office settings by encouraging the proliferation of cheap puns for bracket names (it's part of the NCAA's marketing strategy). Puns are great — you can get a ton of mileage out of them. I did a quick scan, and in about .9 seconds here's what I found for bracket puns from last year's tournament: Full Metal Bracket, Final Fourgasm, Zion King, Hoops There It Is, This Whole Thing's A Bracket…hilarious! And that's just .9 seconds' worth!

Okay, it's not that good, maybe the bracket name thing is a dud, forget I brought it up.

What about how betting on college basketball in March just makes people clinically insane? Billionaire investor Warren Buffett, a longtime basketball fan, singlehandedly offered his Berkshire Hathaway employees $1 million a year for life if they could guess which teams made it to the Sweet 16. Meanwhile, it's estimated 70 million brackets are filled out each year, with $10.4 billion wagered in total — greater than the GDP of many countries. But here's the best part: particularly in office settings, the time spent focused on bracketology rather than work during the NCAA Tournament is estimated to be worth $6.3 billion in corporate *losses*.

But it's good for morale and stuff. Can you imagine capturing those gains and then distributing them to employees as fair portioning of…oh never mind, I won't go there.

Finally, what about the horrible rage March Madness induces when some dolt who threw in five bucks and barely pays attention during the intense two-week tournament 'cause he's too busy chillin' and kicking it with cool people you wish you knew wins the whole thing? Or the intern wins? Or that guy who's always sucking up to the boss? Or the little old lady who won't retire, which makes you mad because you want her parking space? Fantasy Football rage just doesn't compare to March Madness rage — it can't. The emotional journey of Fantasy Football is too long and spread out with lots of ups and downs; March Madness compresses all that energy into one big blast of obsessive competition, complete with either a screaming, rocket-fueled launch to massive heights or a dizzying, stomach-churning drop to dreadful, going-to-have-to-sell-your-car-to-cover-the-spread depths.

Okay, no one really gets mad at little old ladies who win massive betting pools. I don't think.

The point of all this is for you to accept my assertion that it's March. It is. You can deny it all you want, but it is. And since it's March, things are about to get really crazy. I hope you're ready. A good way to prepare is to start your day with a Shamrock Shake. Go for it. It's on me.

I'D LOVE TO VISIT A STADIUM SOMETIME SOON

WINTER 2021

Opening weekend for the 2021 Major League Soccer (MLS) season is set for April 3-4, 2021! Thank God.

Those of us in the Pacific Northwest know this means the Sounders FC will soon take the pitch, and to a lesser degree, if one lives in a certain sales-tax-free state on the southern border of Magnificent Washington, so will the Portland Timbers. Regardless of what a dumb name that is.

The story nobody is talking about, however, is the impending league-wide cancellation of all matches scheduled for Sunday, April 4, what with coaches and managers predicting that a majority of their first team players will be napping all day after gorging themselves on quiche Lorraine, spiral-sliced Honey Baked Ham, cheesy potatoes, and sticky buns. Or whatever they choose to eat

for Easter brunch, regardless of religious affil-
iation, but noting the fact that people just love
to eat a big brunch. With breakfast cocktails.
Followed by naps.

I offered to be a midfielder that day, but no one
at the Sounders ever returns my calls.

Time capsules are interesting things, and it's
worth noting that (roughly) a year ago today, MLS
suspended the 2020 season. Of course, matches
essentially, eventually, restarted, and even
though history, statistics, reporters, and others
will state FC Columbus won the 2020 MLS Cup, I
know this is a scandalous lie secondary to a
massive conspiracy and the Sounders actually won.
It was great. I was invited to the after-party
and everything.

It's quite amazing the season happened at all,
considering I spent the majority of this time
last year anticipating the sudden closure of
planet Earth and therefore panic-bought beer on a
daily basis (particularly from local brewery
stars Matchless, Fremont, Reubens, Great Notion...
mmmmmmm), repeated this for several weeks, then
noticed that by late May I (a) had gained 20
pounds and (b) hadn't lost access to any micro-
brewery's points of distribution.

At least I know where my priorities are.

So the Sounders and all of MLS were back, are
back, and will be back again starting in April.
But it's not the same organization. Speaking with
a colleague who happens to understand the busi-

ness operations of the club, I discovered some fascinating details about what impacts COVID made on the organization, and what sports mean to us.

The MLS business model is a function of revenue generated by the combination of season ticket and regular sales, a.k.a. "butts in seats." The Sounders have a particular advantage in this arena thanks to Lumen Field and its gargantuan-ness. (Many clubs have teeny-tiny fields that only generate about $5.53 in revenue per game, so those of you with ample stadiums should rejoice in your fortune). Meanwhile, with no butt-warmed seats to be found in any stadium, rumor has it club owners league-wide are continuing to lose absurd amounts of money but can still cover their losses, and are doing so for the sake of their employees.

What? Capitalism doing right by actual humans? I know, but I happen to believe that absurd rumor, based on the following juicy insight:

The percentage of overall revenue from home game ticket sales for an MLS team is a lot bigger than in other sports. For example, the NFL has so much TV money involved that any lack of screaming fans inside a given stadium wouldn't (and didn't) derail a season or result in bankruptcies. Thus, with revenue directly tied to people's butts (so many jokes could come from this), every MLS team was in (and may still be in) a really tough spot and set to lose more revenue than other sports. The economics just aren't there; they should all be done, over, closed. Enter billionaire owners.

It has to be the billionaires doling out some scratch to cover the losses that's keeping MLS afloat. See? They're not all bad, those crazy billionaires with their caviar breakfasts and full-scale backyard amusement parks.

Of course, last year's season wasn't without its painful cuts. Soccer programs, including recreational soccer, summer camps, and the youth club development program, were eliminated, much to the distress of up-and-coming players and particularly their parents, who likely wondered just what in the hell they were going to do with their bouncy-ass, wound-up, hyper kids all summer. Well, spring and summer. There's also a midwinter break camp, but that was in the rearview mirror by the time COVID hit.

The loss of these programs may seem trivial, but it's actually a pretty big deal for outreach and connection, the latter of which is now officially the most valuable commodity in the world. Not only do sports programs keep kids healthy (and parents sane), but in this case access to first team players is a big deal for any kid aspiring to do the soccer thing. I mean, imagine being a kid (or in my case adult) and meeting your hero, then having them be your COACH. I'd probably pass out.

There was, of course, an attempt to pivot to a digital soccer program experience — with the Sounders' videography team creating and shipping to families content featuring the beloved first team players — but as with various schools' first attempts at distance learning, engagement was low since execution relied on heavy parental involvement. And those fools be working from home and just don't have the *time* for that.

There's a chance soccer programs will come back in 2022, but given that MLS soccer has to generate its revenue by putting the first team product on the field, selling the stadium, and selling season tickets, it's unlikely.

Which leaves some folks within MLS — particularly those whose job it is to foster public interaction with the teams through various real-life programs — in quite a predicament. It's very similar to what many small business owners, particularly in the food and beverage industry, face if they have to close or sell their business: the need to find work. After all, these folks' careers are based on their ability to create connection and a remarkable experience by building something from nothing. Anyone hiring for that?

People will one day fill stadiums and arenas again, and any sport is excited for this. It's the definition of fun —experiencing something you love with 40,000 other people shoulder to shoulder is what makes sports so special. It's the commodity of connection, which turns out to be the most valuable commodity we've had all along.

SHOTGUN SPORTS AND STEAKS ARE THE BEST

WINTER 2021

Since I'm really into self-delusion, I enjoy fishing, hunting, and the gentlemanly sport of blasting the bejeezus out of clay pigeons. There's no better place to blast the bejeezus out of clay pigeons than the booming metropolis of Sequim, Washington.

And when I say "no better place," I really mean it. I don't care where you're from. Looking at you, Beaverton, Oregon.

Okay, Sequim's not exactly booming in a metropolitan way, more like in a shooting sporting clays at Sunnydell Shooting Grounds way. If you've never been to a "shooting grounds" you should go, because the sport of shooting inanimate objects is as enjoyable as a round of golf, a match of tennis, a game of darts, the supposedly pleasurable activity called hiking...you know, all those activities we do to have fun. Shooting is just way louder.

Wait, this is already out of control. Before we move on, it's possible you, the avid, storied reader, need some definitions and clarifications. No problem.

1. Self-delusion is defined as failing to recognize reality. Fishing/hunting/shooting can be used to further define this mental state, given the lopsided expense/success ratio. E.g., if you factor in all your gear, lures, fuel, etc., that seven-pound salmon you caught in Puget Sound last summer cost you $4,888.50, or $698.35 per pound.

2. Clay pigeons are little ceramic frisbees one shoots with a shotgun in an attempt to generate a sense of self-worth.

3. Sporting clays, a.k.a. "golf with a shotgun," involves several shooting stations embedded in natural terrain and hurling clay pigeons at impossible speeds/angles. This frustrating hobby was, quite deviously, invented by the American Psychological Association to increase global demand for cognitive therapy sessions.

Sunnydell has quite the storied history and is such a great place to shoot that maybe you should stop reading this now because I'm suddenly para-noid the next time I go you're all going to be there, taking up space and generally getting in the way like all new people do. Especially me when I'm new, I'm the worst.

Oh fine. Chuck Dryke established Sunnydell in 1967, trained many successful trap and skeet shooters, including his daughter Ellen (competed in Shotgun World Championships) and son Matt (competed in three Olympics, winning a gold medal for skeet shooting in 1984), and pioneered the science behind how to "see" targets.

I've taken lessons from Chuck (who passed away in 2012 at the age of 88), Matt, and another instructor I can't remember. I've also received plenty of guidance from Ellen. By the end of a lesson you will be making impossible shots — I guarantee it, unless you're a poor listener or insist on talking over the instructor, which really drives me nuts, as in why are you even paying for that lesson when all you want to do is prattle on about your problems or your Tesla or what you think about anything? Just listen for once.

Sorry.

After a lesson I can hit anything I want for about a week, then it wears off, kind of like my charm. For the record it wears off mostly because I live in a dense metropolitan area that discourages discharging shotguns at clay targets in 2,000-square-foot backyards, so I can't keep practicing. Plus maybe I'm not what you'd call a "natural." Which also explains why, as my wife keeps noting, I always come back from duck hunting with no ducks (see above definition of self-delusion.)

I've seen instructors shoot a shotgun one-handed and break targets at 30 yards. I've watched our out-of-town guests who haven't shot in 10 years have a great time shooting "teal" (a clay pigeon launched vertically in the air), "rabbit" (one that bounces and skips across the ground), and a crazy one that actually comes toward you from across a pond. I think that last station is called "angry raptor attacking you," and it's pretty much about self-defense.

It turns out I kind of take Sunnydell for granted. If you do a little research and talk to a few of the folks who take shotgunning seri- ously, or even professionally, you'll find they view Sunnydell as one of the best sporting-clays ranges in the world, and certainly top-rated nationally.

Plus when you're done at the shooting grounds, your hands smell like cordite (think pungent, earthy/rust smell, I really find it quite agree- able, as I do gun oil), you crave steak (a biological response to blasting the bejeezus out of clay pigeons), and your shoulder hurts just a bit. Then when you see your friends at work on Monday and you're like, "Whadja do this weekend?" and they're like, "We went to this new tapas restaurant oh it was so good and we had so many fifteen-dollar cocktails" and they say that all nasally and boring, then they ask you what you did, you get to say, "Oh we went to Sequim, you know, with my [insert noun here…girl-friend/boyfriend/family/wife/dog…whatever] and we shot sporting clays at the shooting equivalent of a training ground for world champions, ate a bunch of meat, and my shoulder still kind of hurts. From the shooting, not from eating the meat."

And you'll obviously win that conversation because your story is way cooler than your coworker's. And you might get a raise that day because everyone at work will be talking about how awesome you are, and your boss will finally really notice you and think you're a real avant-garde go-getter. And you'll feel obligated to send me some of your new raise money because really you have me to thank since I pointed you in the right direction with this whole shooting sports thing in the first place. See? Why didn't you start listening to me a long time ago? Oh, and I guess you could thank Matt and Ellen and Sunnydell in general if you want.

And, most importantly, thank Chuck Dryke, who, as many other writers have suggested, is likely in heaven teaching angels how to shoot their golden bows in a much more excellent manner. Or something like that.

IT'S OKAY TO ALREADY BE THINKING ABOUT SUMMER SPORTS

SPRING 2021

Even though we're only in March, and technically the first day of spring was just last weekend, and Pacific Northwest springs aren't very spring-like until about May, and right now it's freezing outside, and raining, and I'm hungry — there are some summer sporting activities that I simply cannot wait to see again, as outlined below, don't stop now you're almost there you should read this.

I mean, it would be a shame if something happened to that nice car of yours, so go ahead and have a seat and let's get on with it:

Public-Access Golf — Nothing screams "summer" as much as a completely burnt fairway on a public course with literally no barrier to entry, fence or otherwise. My favorite pastime is to listen to the brown, highly flammable grass crunch under my feet as I hack my way through an 18-hole course, utilizing my dad's circa 1977 leather golf bag, seven clubs, a case of golf balls, 12 Miller High Lifes, and my phone turned off because my wife thinks I'm at Home Depot buying supplies to fix our fence.

Boozy Softball Games — I don't enjoy sweating, and even though serious adult softball leagues are filled with ex-varsity athletes who somehow still have something to prove, the reality is softball is a joke sport that shouldn't be taken too seriously or produce perspiration. Thus, I enjoy watching the super casual leagues, typically coed, where the outfield consumes alcohol in red Solo cups during the game in the form of beer, or maybe one of those canned Moscow Mule or other premixed drinks that are all over the place and conveniently look like soda. Anyway, my kind of outfield can't be bothered to shag foul balls or cover a base.

Or sweat. Note: I said I enjoy watching these games. Like from the benches or maybe lying in the dirt. Not playing in them.

"NO HORSEPLAY" Signs at Pools and "NO DIVING" Signs at Waterparks — Or really any restrictive signage around things people enjoy, like pools and water parks. This stems from the fact that part of me is a huge advocate for increased caution and safety around things that are wet, while the other part basically appreciates anything that prevents people from having a better time than me, regardless of what I'm doing, or they're doing.

Boozy Disc Golf — I used to work with a guy who was so into disc golf he would tear out of work at 900 miles an hour at quitting time, and I swear he played disc golf right up to the moment he had to return the next morning. It was weird, to the point that I hoped he did it just so he could get stoned versus having that level of obsession for the actual activity. I've never played disc golf or seen it played, other than the time we were at a social distance-friendly park a few months back on a rare sunny Seattle winter day and I saw these nerds throwing impossibly small saucers at Disc Pole Holes, which is the absolutely hilarious name for the sport's catching device, consisting of 10 chains hanging in a parabolic shape over an upward-opening basket. Anyway, they looked like they were having fun, but not too much fun, so I thereby support this behavior.

Dogfish — Beware: Along with the blistering 68° heat of a Pacific Northwest summer come the dogfish. These are miniature sharks that swarm our ocean beaches and inland waters as they migrate from God-knows-where, probably near Anaheim, in search of shark girlfriends and boyfriends with which to perform slightly buoyant, kinky sex acts. If you fish for salmon in salt water, you're likely familiar with these beasts' razor-sharp teeth and preternatural ability to chomp your leader in half. Dogfish may be the one animal I've never heard anyone attempt to throw conservation at. Folks are probably like, "Yeah, those things? We're good on those."

Zombie Fish — When salmon spawn, they die. It's a weird process, kind of like what happens to third-party candidates, as the animals steadily decompose in motion. If you fish certain rivers in Oregon and Washington in the heat of summer and you stay sober when passing over some gravel shallows, you get to see the black-and-white, desiccated, skin-peeled zombie salmon hovering over the crop circle—like indentations of their nests, presumably establishing the foundation for some future salmon I'll be eating. Er, fishing for. Or maybe they're just being dramatic about their deaths, I don't know.

Watching People Do CrossFit from a Bar — Most CrossFit places in my general area somehow have indoor/outdoor facilities. I guess what I'm saying is they have parking lots, and front doors that open, which now that I think of it really isn't a big deal. Anyway, CrossFit enthusiasts smack of extroversion or fitness obsession, two qualities I, as a slightly overweight introvert, find quite irritating. If you're lucky enough, however, to have a burger joint with a bar across the street from a CrossFit gym, let me assure you nothing beats sitting outside in the sun with two or three pints and a double bacon cheeseburger maybe with some jalapeños and a side of onion rings, and watching these lunatics push themselves to their physical limits in said parking lots. One day soon, I too will seek to push my physical limits again without involving bacon, cheese, or a fryer.

Maybe by the end of summer.

OPENING DAY FOR LITTLE LEAGUE DRAMA

SPRING 2021

Last year Seattle's North Central Little League cancelled its baseball season, which was tragic for kids aged 7 to 13. More importantly, it was devasting for their hypercompetitive parents, whose entire existence is predicated on sacrificing their overall familial relationship for the sake of future stardom and financial gain. Or at least a scholarship.

And don't forget those poor coaches with no one to yell at.

Okay, not all coaches yell, and admittedly it's a tough business. Coaching kids' sports takes quite a bit of patience, resilience, and a hole in your life you're trying to fill by winning what amounts to a truly inconsequential game. I mean, it's inconsequential statistics-wise — of course, the kids learn how to be part of a team, develop self-esteem, build resilience, etc., etc. If you think that's important.

But when it comes to baseball, coaching takes an unbelievable amount of time. This is because a standard Little League game/practice takes upwards of 14 hours, what with the walks and the beanballs and the nose-picking and the grass-examining and spontaneous outbreaks of wrestling. And that's just the obvious stuff — don't forget about stopping everything because the ball went into the street or onto the front lawn of that grumpy neighbor who's completely flabbergasted by the fact that people are on his property despite his living right next to a park.

Speaking of delays, there's also that dreaded "I'm running late" text from a truant parent so the coach has to sit with Billy what's-his-name on the bleachers for an extra 30 minutes after practice when all he really wants to do is go home and drink a beer in the shower.

Or so I hear.

Actually, I know about all this. In 2019 my friend Josh asked me to be an assistant Little League coach for the third year in a row. I reminded him that I (a) don't like baseball other than attending three Mariners games per year, preferably on sunny days, preferably with beer, hot dogs, and nachos, (b) was a terrible baseball player as a child, and (c) have no particular, specific skill to impart other than teaching the underperforming batters to call lots of time-outs at the plate in hopes of getting the pitcher off track (plus it's fun to knock the infield dirt off your cleats like the major leaguers do).

It didn't matter. Once again, Josh needed a living body, and I qualified.

The 2019 season was our first foray into real Little League baseball as the kids were old enough to be in the "Majors" division and thus face serious physical injury. I'd previously helped with T-ball (talk about a snoozefest, but at least it required minimal effort) and what to me is the perfect division, the "Minors."

The Minors was great fun — the kids showed a modicum of respect for authority while still being too small to generate much velocity when pitching/throwing/hitting so you didn't have to pay too much attention. Plus to keep the game moving the coaches took over pitching after ball four (I think), which gave the kids an actual opportunity to hit said ball. Also, the parents were only on the verge of psychotic behavior — you could see them just barely restraining them-selves from screaming about how to coach, how to ump, or (if at the child) how to get an NCAA Division I baseball scholarship.

Minors' practices were the absolute best and involved hitting lots of pop flies to the kids, who comically scrambled and tripped and bumped into each other as they tried to catch/run from the ball. I think this was also the last division that could be coed, which is a shame because it's always fun to watch preternaturally talented girl athletes just absolutely smoke the boys — which hopefully taught those dirty chocolate- and booger-covered mongrels something about diversity and inclusion.

There was, however, a storm on the horizon. At the end of our Minors season I remember casually walking up to an ump I'd never met at a field we'd never played on and asking him if I could stand in the back of the outfield to help coach my kids like I'd done all season. His response was to literally size me up, stretch to his full 6'4" height with all his battle robot umpire gear jangling, and state, "Not in my ballpark," with his hands on his hips all squared-off like he wanted a fistfight or to mount me, I'm not sure which. I responded, "Thank you, you've been very helpful" and walked away realizing the kids had grown big enough to enter a new era, and I wasn't going to like it.

Indeed, the storm we faced the following season was the Majors division, and it was no joke. At our first practice these kids who looked like they should be shaving showed up and threw the ball so hard I thought my hand was going to explode. And their batting stances indicated that yes indeed their fathers were former serious players, one of whom had another son actually playing NCAA Division I baseball, and Josh and I were screwed as our whole coaching philosophy focused on learning and having fun, which suddenly had no place here.

It didn't take long to realize the extent of our doomed-ness. Our team, which the kids had named

"The Fighting Chinchillas" the previous year, now went by the unfortunate moniker "CubeSmart," thanks to that classic feature of neighborhood Americana where local businesses show their community support and increase brand awareness at a relatively cheap rate by sponsoring youth sports teams. CubeSmart builds brand new buildings that at first look like nice condominiums, but it turns out they're just nice apartments for the stuff that won't fit in your house (or micro-condo, or rental), which seems to be the polar opposite of sustainability. When you think about it.

Then, of course, the hierarchy of actual baseball skills became readily apparent to everyone involved. There were five really talented kids on the team, five decent athletes who could sort of keep up, and five terrible players. You could tell the terrible players because at the end of practice or a game they were the ones with blood on their faces, bruised arms, and instant chemical ice packs all over their bodies, thanks to that hardball repeatedly smacking them as they batted/played catch/fielded/walked back to the dugout.

The attrition rate for terrible players the previous year was 0%. This year it was 75%.

The next sign of the apocalypse came when one dad insisted on calling me "Coach," like all the time, despite my protests, to the point where I offered him the gig as it really seemed like he wanted the job — or at least to be called "Coach" himself. Then this other dad volunteered to help as our second assistant coach, but he was gone for the first three games, and when he showed up in the middle of game four he totally lost it when he realized CubeSmart had amassed a 0—3 record in his absence. His mood did not improve when he realized I had benched his (all-star) son in the middle of this game so another kid could get some playing time.

And I mean he like really freaked out. I thought his head was going to explode when he saw the philosophy behind my batting order as well. (Secretly, I had no philosophy.)

We kind of bumbled through the rest of the season, and this dad became the de facto head coach, which was actually great for a while as he really knew his stuff and made a great effort to impart actual skill-developing drills into our practices, which the kids definitely benefited from. The End arrived, however, with three games left in the season, as we came to terms with our 3—7 record and tensions ran high. During practice this same gentleman got into a shouting match with one of our parents over how her kid wasn't playing any position other than right field, which is the graveyard position where you stick horrible players (I should know; I spent five seasons in right field).

I wasn't there for the argument, but I heard about it, and when I saw her at the next practice I explained the dude "is a hard charger but means well," to which this very Philadelphian woman responded with a series of very vocal criticisms, mixed with the occasional profanity the coach's wife and parents (who were apparently visiting) overheard.

Ugh.

I didn't think much of it as there were only two weeks of practices and games left, but this gentleman must have been informed there was a conspiracy against him as he absolutely stopped talking to me, and actually wouldn't even stand near me. Which I'm used to from my social life but was surprised to experience in the context of kids' sports.

And the "hey, Coach" guy stopped saying "hey, Coach" all the time as well, which was somewhat of a relief actually.

To make matters worse, we accidentally won our second-to-last game when these guys were gone and Josh and I put our crappier players in key defensive positions like shortstop. I think the "I'm not talking to you" coach took it personally, but really, like my batting order, my "strategy" was based on absolutely nothing.

Our 2019 Majors season simply ended, and that was the last time I've coached baseball. Usually I'm willing to try things again, but it hasn't come up, and if asked I'd definitely decline. Everything has a time and place, and as time passes, sometimes we get evolved out of a situation. And that's not a bad thing.

But I did enjoy watching the kids play. Baseball is a great sport for just hanging out, and after being in my house all winter the prospect of sitting in the sun and watching the Mariners is extra appealing — I'm glad today is Opening Day.

IF YOU BOOK NOW YOU'LL GET THAT CAMPSITE IN AUGUST 2022

SPRING 2021

I often wonder what it's like to camp in Arizona. Do people just go out into the middle of the Sonoran Desert, pitch a tent, then get eaten by rattlesnakes? Or die of heat stroke? Or freeze? The ground looks extra hard in Arizona, sounds terrible.

Scientific Fact: The Pacific Northwest is full of avid campers. Dome tent campers. Pup tent campers. Bell tent campers. GFC Platform campers. Ozark Trail 8-Person Instant Hexagon Tent model #6121 campers. (There's plenty of space for product placement, give us a call to see your brand here, we're running a spring special).

But let's delineate between camping and what you think also counts as camping but you're dead wrong.

Scientific Fact: Merriam-Webster defines camping as sleeping in a tent. If you're not sleeping under some kind of enclosed fabric structure, a.k.a. you're in a hammock or lying on the ground, you're simply at a Widespread Panic concert, or possibly Phish but I think they broke up.

Similarly, if you're in an RV, travel trailer, Winnebago, motor home, fifth wheel, or God forbid one of those Mercedes-Benz Sprinter or Weekender vans, you're not camping, you're vacationing.

Same rules apply to the biggest poseur of all camping, "car camping." Don't walk around bragging about how you and your non-uptight family spontaneously went to "Moab" to go "car camping" again, the whole neighborhood is sick of it, okay? And you're not even using the proper, globally accepted, international understanding of car camping. For global purposes, car camping is literally what happens when you sleep in your car, *anywhere*, rather than your narrowly defined "going to a place where you can drive your car right up to the campsite and park next to the provided bench and firepit, then pitch your tent and pile up all your other gear."

Think of it like this: When you wake up at the curb of Swizzle Rum Bar & Drinkery off Florida State Road A1A or, internationally, on Rue de Rivoli after a rough night at the Louvre, you're car camping, which is fine, because you shouldn't be driving after going to those places. But you should know you can still technically get a ticket (or arrested) based on the municipal code of most…municipalities and how they look poorly upon drunk people in vehicles. As they should.

Where are we? The point is, car camping doesn't count.

We realize you are now terribly confused. This is normal with the realization you are a complete and utter camping phony. Or maybe you're just confused. We'll set you straight.

Real campers do the following:

- Hang out exclusively in ridge tents, dome tents, geodesic tents, tunnel tents, inflatable tents…even at work; it's weird
- Shop exclusively at REI and hope they're seen doing so (they're never seen)
- Insist on bringing along their boyfriends, girlfriends, dog friends, husbands, wives, kids, in-laws…despite your insistence that there's not enough room or you simply hate those people
- Cook with camp stoves, raw fire, cast-iron Dutch ovens, Chef Master® 3-piece Portable Single Burner Butane Ranges (click here for a limited-time offer of two ranges for $36.99)
- Make shrimp foil boils, chicken tzatziki skewers, campfire nachos, campfire popcorn, campfire pizza, campfire coffee, campfire griddle cakes (starting to see a trend here), something called banana boats (maybe it has something to do with the final

bullet), and, of course, napalm-like roasted marshmallows

- Don't mind pooping in the woods
- Incessantly smoke weed as this is the only thing that makes camping bearable
- Have loose sex with whoever else is at the campground or within six square miles because all campers are kinky sex swingers (Scientific Fact)
- Are always covered with about 1/16th of an inch of dirt, emphasized by the trail of sweat from last night's insect-filled forage for firewood carved down the center of their dirty forehead so they look like a skunk with a misplaced stripe
- Have weird little rituals in the woods involving chakras
- Secondary to the above, believe in woodland "faeries"
- Drink water, beer, soda, mountain margaritas, wine, Bloody Mary Muds (real name), cinnamon hot buttered rum, and various DIY premixed cocktails to the point we think we should tell them they have a problem
- Bathe in creeks, lakes, ponds, portable shower tents, and if really wealthy solar showers, oftentimes cavorting around nakedly in large groups as they do so, much to the delight of any nearby, isolated, and extremely lonely Park Rangers — all in preparation for more campground sex
- Put all their cookware right back in the garage upon returning home, and it just

sits there and kind of rots because all
they did was wash it in a salmonella-filled
creek with some Dawn® Dishwashing Liquid's
new Platinum Formula but the grease is
still there, and maybe a few bits of
potatoes, the perfect recipe for black
mold, how gross

- Never invite us back for some reason,
possibly because we complain, and we're
scared of the spooky noises nature makes at
night

If, based on your experience, all of these points
don't apply to you, we hate to break it to you,
but we want to go out with somebody else. It's
not you, it's us. We're just not in a good place
right now and...ah, we mean, you're not an actual
camper. We don't know what the hell you are —
maybe a hiker, or an addict, or delusional — but
you're no camper.

Welcome to summer.

BEAR CRAWLS BOLSTER NATIONAL SECURITY

SPRING 2021

When I was a freshman in high school, my first class of the first semester was physical education (P.E.) at 7:45 a.m. Somehow I drew the same short straw my sophomore year. How I envied the kids who enjoyed P.E. at roughly 1:00 p.m., in the daylight, with actual waves of radiant heat emanating from the sun — they had it so good.

I recall suffering through various freezing activities (even the buildings' interiors were cold; I think they used a gigantic, Freddy Kruegeresque, fire-driven central boiler built in 1949 to heat the campus as it took all day to gain any efficacy), including these delights:

- Watching the football players excel at flag football, much to the satisfaction of our very tight sweatshort-wearing P.E.

teachers, Mr. Reeves and Mr. Pica, who pulled double duty as the Head Football and Assistant Football Coaches, respectively.

- Watching the football players excel at weight lifting, including utilizing forms since deemed inadvisable by health and fitness professionals, like yarding down on the lat pull bar to the base of your neck (behind your head) with as much weight as possible to the point it sort of lifted you off the ground. And using an actual "neck machine" to kind of torque your neck forward and backward, ostensibly to strengthen and/or tear your neck ligaments, apparently.
- Watching the football players excel at this horrible game called "knee rugby,"* where you run around on your knees on wrestling mats and try to throw a rugby ball into a floor hockey net "goal" while getting absolutely mauled by football players. And wrestlers.

*In order to survive knee rugby,** my friends and I developed a plan where we avoided the "scrum" (a.k.a. big pile of sweaty, hairy bodies piled on top of each other with hands awkwardly probing for/ripping at the "prize" rugby ball thing) by kind of halfheartedly milling around its perimeter and grunting/growling loudly caveman-style in an effort to fake both our enthusiasm and participation.

**The goal was to signal to the coaches that we were, yes indeed, violence-prone American boys eager to kill each other simply for possession of the inflated, inanimate elliptical object and thus earn ourselves a proper place within the tribe (and receive some form of beneficial grade). And possibly allow them to rest assured that our great nation would survive any attack by the Soviet Union, nuclear or otherwise, thanks to the strength and fortitude and bloodlust of its Young Men. I mean, the Cold War was still going on and stuff, so it was likely on their minds.

Of course, P.E. wasn't just about football play-ers. Sometimes we played volleyball, where the basketball players excelled.

Interestingly enough, we never actually played basketball. I wonder if somebody was basketball-murdered during class and they had to sweep the incident under the rug, under an agreement with the School Board to never speak of it, or play of it, again?

One of the most bizarre activities involved training for that stupid President's Challenge Physical Fitness Award, promulgated by the Presi-dent's Council on Sports, Fitness and Nutrition (actual government agency thing). This crucible was introduced by Lyndon B. Johnson in 1966 in an effort to encourage all Americans to "make being active part of their everyday lives and be physi-cally fit and stop being such fat, burger-eating slobs."

(Talk about a thin veil, this was surely instituted to create a population stalwart enough to survive a Soviet attack — Johnson likely had a hotline to Mr. Reeves and Mr. Pica and all P.E. teachers across the nation so he could receive weekly readiness updates on young America's ability to repel Evil Communist Invaders. I wonder if he also had a pair of tight sweatshorts he wore around the Oval Office.)

The "challenges" (one had to score in the 85th percentile in each to achieve the award) included curl-ups, pull-ups, push-ups, the sit-and-reach, the 30-foot shuttle run, and the one-mile endurance run.

> **Little-Known Fact:** If you made a contribution to the Democratic Party you only had to score in the 50th percentile.

> **Another Little-Known Fact:** If you could demonstrate proficiency in attacking a series of fortified communist bunkers by calling in artillery then conducting a squad-level assault by laying down a base of fire then flanking the position, you only had to score in the 10th percentile.

Despite being forced to routinely practice these activities throughout the semester, I didn't score in the 85th percentile in any of them when it came to test time. Well, at least not the push-ups and pull-ups. But due to a clerical error, upon graduation I received the little gold tassel thing that indicated I was an Official Award Recipient. I didn't say anything.

I just read that the program was discontinued on June 30, 2018, because the Presidential Administration at the time deemed the private sector to be whipping young folks into shape just fine. I actually blame today's young people themselves, what with their propensity for having good relationships with their parents, holding corporations accountable for creating a greater good for society and the planet, refusing to smoke, and other bewildering habits that promote health and wellness, both physically and mentally. They didn't need help from the feds.

Another unique task we, particularly as freshmen, had to complete to get into the good graces of our very square-jawed, violence-loving instructors involved running the interior perimeter of the gym, then "bear crawling" the same perimeter, then running again, and so on and so forth, then dying.

Bear crawling is basically crawling in a push-up position. I see it's regained popularity amongst extremist groups, including Bootcamp enthusiasts, ACE-certified personal trainers, the Taliban, and bears — particularly the aggressive packs of black bears continuing to encroach on our fragile urban spaces that the woods keep sprawling over as we just simply try to exist and build driveways for Amazon drivers to park in/future drones to land in so they can deliver our Very Important Items® that much faster.

Anyway, bear crawling is a nightmare (although it does explain bears' impressive abs), and I still have post-traumatic stress over the whole thing. Occasionally the P.E. teaching assistants would encourage one's effort by threatening to strike one as one's bear crawling effort lagged (due to a combination of dehydration, exhaustion, and cardiac arrhythmia) — coupled with occasional actual strikes. Accompanied by hollow, synapse-free, mouth-only, hyena-type laughter from what can only be described as an actual, legitimate, hopeless doofus of a teaching assistant. Not that I'm bitter. Besides, it was the very late '80s, so physical abuse and bullying were socially acceptable.   HisnamewasPatTooeyandIhatehim...pant, pant.

So that was physical education in the late '80s to early '90s: getting tackled, creating permanent deformities with free weights, running weird drills, and generally almost getting killed. Oh! I forgot about the post-class open and completely freezing showers. That was fun.

Nowadays P.E. teachers do all this altruistic stuff to make their students healthier in mind and body. Which is great, mostly because it proves my demographic faced much more adversity and thus developed more resilience than today's teenagers, what with their kale salads, quinoa, and proper strength and conditioning techniques. I mean, do you really think these kids can repel an invading army?

TENNIS IS ALL ABOUT GETTING A GREAT TAN

SPRING 2021

Tennis players are amazing athletes, and amazing people. Just look at Rod Laver. Who is Rod Laver? I have no idea, but he had a Wilson tennis racket named after him, or possibly a pair of shoes, so he must have been double amazing. Or was that Stan Smith?

Let's not enter the boring world of my convincing you how difficult it is to be a good tennis player. But on second thought, let's enter it a little bit — I'll hit you with some fun, granted anecdotal, facts, with no site sourcing, making them almost hearsay, but facts nonetheless:

- The two best tennis players I knew in high school always came in first during any form of fitness test we (entire P.E. class,

including football players) participated
in.

- Tennis is massively aerobic and anaerobic, like running a marathon with frequent, intermittent wind-sprinting (as with basketball, when I play tennis now it serves as the perfect litmus test of how out of shape I am).

- Tennis is massively mental, purely based on the lack of teammates to lean on (max: one, if you play doubles). It's the psychological equivalent of being a kicker in the NFL — it's all good until there's two seconds left and you're on the 35-yard line and there's no statistical reason you should miss and there are 7 yards from the holder who's about to call for the snap but wait was that just a slight gust of wind…?

- Writer David Foster Wallace accurately explains (obviously way better than I ever could) the inherent, mind-numbing-when-you-think-about-it trigonometry and physics involved in the sport, second only to golf, with the following description: *"…shot's depth is determined by the height at which the ball passes over the net combined with some integrated function of pace and spin, with the ball's height over the net itself determined by the player's body position, grip on the racket, degree of backswing, angle of racket face, and that interval in which the ball is actually on the strings."*

Whew. Okay, we're done with that part. You can wake up now.

I played tennis in high school. I don't intend to create a historiography of my storied accomplishments on the court here, mostly because they speak for themselves and are codified in bronze on the northeast corner of the USTA Billie Jean King National Tennis Center in Flushing Meadows, New York, where the U.S. Open Tennis Championships transpire.

Correction. It is now called Flushing Meadows Corona Park. As of 1967. I'm not sure how I missed this. At first I was terrified Corona Extra, as in the Mexican beer, had bought the rights to Flushing Meadows and we were going to have to watch the tournament succumb to six-foot-tall beer bottle inflatables set up across the grounds and in the stands. But it turns out "Flushing" and "Corona" are simply adjacent communities.

I have a right to be paranoid about this stuff — somehow corporations are the only entities with enough cash to buy stadium signs with which to increase brand awareness. CenturyLink Field here in Seattle now goes by Lumen Field, which is just the new name for CenturyLink, a telecommunications monopoly/robber baron. And Safeco Field is now T-Mobile Park (yawn; T-Mobile is a telecommunications company that hires a lot of people around here although my understanding is it's quite boring to work there). And the old KeyArena was recently rechristened Climate Pledge Arena, its website saying it's "the most progressive, responsible and sustainable arena in the world."

Yes, "Climate Pledge Arena, named after a pledge, not a corporation," which is nice, although a somewhat ham-fisted attempt at a name if I do say so. Maybe they were in a hurry. They do have an impressive goal-set when it comes to helping fight climate change. It focuses on operating a gigantic building for people to drive to and watch sports, clearly demonstrating Climate Pledge Arena's intention not to use fossil fuels for daily use. No gas-powered rotating pretzel merchandizers here, no thank you. And even though it's not a "corporate building," Amazon and Alaska Airlines are heavily involved, but that's okay too since they don't use lots of fossil fuels on a daily basis either.

Okay fine, it's the right thing, even if it's 50% marketing, 30% political, and 20% the important part. It's better than 0% the important part.

I will say there is a distinct absence of tennis stadiums in the Pacific Northwest — the only one I can think of is at the University of Washington, and it's more a set of indoor courts with bleacher seating, the kind with little grooves on them that are distinctly uncomfortable to sit on and leave lines on the backs of your thighs, but I haven't been there in 20 years so maybe it got better.

Having actually played tennis for quite a while, I find that my favorite thing about the sport is competing with someone who's a great athlete but maybe never took a lesson and thinks they can just smash the ball around and win because tennis seems to them relatively easy and any difficulty they encounter could be easily overcome by their inherent strength and athleticism. Of course, it doesn't work like that, just like I can't actually golf even though I have decent hand-eye coordination. And I'm sure it applies to other sports as well and, let's face it, comes down to whether you received training as a child. Anyone who spends legitimate time playing golf, tennis, basketball, or baseball between the ages of 6 and 12 is automatically a candidate for at least making the high school varsity team, or otherwise seeming "really good."

I purposefully exclude football from this list because, other than with quarterback, I've witnessed several big strong kids with no playing experience become great football players in high school and even at the University of Washington. You can actually smash your way ahead in that sport because, after all, it's all about smashing. And concussions.

Which brings up an interesting point regarding playing tennis in high school. Despite the talent and athletic ability required, absolutely no one cares. It probably didn't help that in the early '90s we wore teeny little shorts that barely covered our groins and buttocks (à la Rod Laver). I wouldn't want to watch that either. Although we did have some awesome Adidas velour full-length sweatsuits that were back in style thanks to Run-D.M.C. — well, it was like '89 to '92 so maybe they were just recently out of style. Anyway, being on the tennis team made you famous with the 12 other guys on the tennis team. And the coach. And the two team manager girls, who were not interested in you but rather interested in getting the class credit promised for managing the team.

I realize this is well documented, but in the sports hierarchy of high school it basically goes: #1, Football. End. That's it.

Think about it. Football = popularity and cheer-leaders and an entire Friday night devoted to it. Basketball? Eh, a somewhat close second but there's just too many games. Baseball, distant third, it's just a nonstarter; it's like the season begins once school is out. Then there's soccer — which makes it to fourth place only because soccer players get European haircuts and are genetically drawn to high fashion, so that resonates with the crowd to a degree.

Then there's number five: all girls' sports. Sorry, it's true, it's not right, and perhaps à la Climate Pledge Arena the right steps are being taken now so in 30 years we change things.

Finally, in a distant, wayyyyyyyyyyy distant sixth place come cross country, track and field, and tennis, all together.

No fans. No cheerleaders. No credibility for participation.

Two of the guys on my team were really talented. Both went on to play Division I tennis. I don't know what kind of props they got for playing Division I tennis, and just as with any sport (including women's sports!), to make it there you have to be really, really good. But basically during high school they were just seen as some cool dudes. Which is good, I guess, it's just interesting how their excellence didn't make an impact beyond the immediacy of the other guys on the team.

About five years prior to my arrival, our school produced a guy by the name of Pat Galbraith. Maybe not produced, more like "was blessed by the arrival of." I think he won the State Singles Championship all four years. It's hard to find that info because Pat became a professional tennis player specializing in doubles, and his stats are dominated by small things like reaching the World No. 1 doubles ranking in 1993. He won the U.S. Open mixed doubles championship in 1994 and was the men's doubles runner-up at Wimbledon in 1993 and 1994. Plus he did a bunch of other stuff, and I think he's actually the chairperson of the U.S. Open tennis tournament these days.

And I'm pretty sure he wore the same (literally the same) Adidas full-length velour Run-D.M.C. sweatsuits we did (I don't think the tennis team budget was given much priority — I guess it makes sense for the football players to have updated pads and helmets since the risk of physical harm is so much greater in that sport).

Maybe Pat and the team got some attention when he played, not sure. He's far and away the best

player I've ever seen in real life. It's unreal
how he moved, anticipated, generated velocity…
it's like the one time I had super-close-to-
courtside seats at an NBA game — my feet have
literally never moved as fast as those dudes'.

Anyway, the takeaway for you is to maybe go out
and hit tennis balls on some court this summer,
regardless of how terrible you are. It's pretty
fun, you get a tan and a great workout, and if
somebody really good happens to be playing next
to you, you'll have a better idea of what I'm
talking about. Feel free to wear full-length or
at least normal-length shorts, though — those
teeny-tiny ones are hard to move around in.

A GEOLOGIC RECORD OF
RAMPANT SEXISM

SPRING 2021

The 2021 Trout Derby, put on by the Washington State Department of Fish and Wildlife (WDFW), opened Saturday, April 24th.

Who doesn't like a derby? When was the last time you were in any kind of derby — go-kart, fishing, horse race, or otherwise? 1959? I thought the word was extinct. We should put on a derby together, you and me. Some weird new kind of derby. No sex stuff, though. Why do you always have to go straight to the sex stuff?

Anyway, what WDFW does is partner with about 70 businesses to create some cash prizes represented by miniature orange tags they brutally staple onto the trout's teeny-tiny little fins — you can hear the trout screams clearly emanating from the genetic engineering factories they're imprisoned in, deep in the woods, during the weeks prior to the event. The WDFW folk wear big leather aprons and creepy masks and everything, it's a super weird agency. Just saying.

So you getta the tag, you getta the prize. Which is why I've invested in 20,000 orange tags in total, with fifteen size and shape variants coupled with 79 water-resistant fonts, in an effort to scam the whole system, much in the way Washington State Employment Security got scammed out of $600 million by that international fraud scheme out of Nigeria during the beginning of the pandemic. Not long after which the head of that agency, Suzi Levine, somehow got promoted to a job with the Biden Administration.

Speaking of career moves, lately I've been encouraging my 12-year-old son to go into meteorology, especially here in the Pacific Northwest, because outside of baseball it's one of the few industries where you can "miss" 70% of the time and not only keep your job but be considered for promotion/pay raises/general advancement. Maybe I'll advise him to look into working for Employment Security as well, not that I think he's incompetent.

Where were we? Oh! The WDFW Trout Derby ties directly to the "Lowland Lakes Season Opener" — i.e., it's a way for the State to advertise that you can now buy a license for the 2021-2022 fishing season and go catch some trout. And bass. And perch. And with some additional coin some salmon, later in the summer, when the season starts — as well as crab. Yum. Oh, and razor clams.

Which reminds me of two insane guys I know who like to fish for surf perch and dig razor clams. It works like this:

- Drive to the Washington, or possibly Oregon, coast. Although if you go to Oregon you have to watch out for the gas stations because they get real mad when you try and pump your own gas. They'll come out and stop you and everything. Literally no one knows why.
- If digging razor clams, your drive and overall activity may take place in the middle of the night, in a pelting rainstorm with gale-force winds, because accessing the clams is directly related to the tide, and humans have yet to learn how to control supernatural forces like tides, although Elon Musk is working on it.
- Oh, the razor clam season is announced almost without warning, it lasts for like a day, then closes, then a week later reopens; somehow it's related to either conservation or WDFW employees wanting lots of time off (which is why I'm also encouraging my son to explore a career with this department).
- When fishing for surf perch — and this may blow your mind — put on some chest waders (it's like wearing a human-sized condom), or

if you're a real badass don't, then walk into the surf with your (you guessed it) surf-casting pole and take a bunch of breakers to your face as you cast and retrieve for hours on end, hoping to snag one of the (delicious) little beasts. Which are prone to attacking your feet in huge swarms, just warning you.

- I think this perch thing can happen in the middle of the night too, not sure, but my friend Rick said he does it at certain tidal moments, which again we cannot yet dictate the behavior of. Come on, Elon, you've got this!

Once you've filled your hand-woven seagrass basket with this ocean bounty, gather your family around on the beach, even though it's 3:00 a.m., start a fire, clean and debeard the clams, fillet the perch, then run to the store to buy some bread and corn and have a good ol' beach picnic. Even if the winds are onshore and blowing at 30 miles per hour. They'll thank you for it later, I promise.

For full disclosure: I'm far too cowardly to participate in such demonstrations of classic rugged American individualism. Which is why my family and I like to go to Sun Lakes-Dry Falls State Park in Washington (this sentence sponsored by Grant County Tourism Council).

Here's the short version of that park's history:

Thirteen thousand years ago it was cold and icy across most of northern North America, 365 days a year. As with Oregon's refusal to let the public pump their own gas, no one knows why. And we're talking really cold — like Vermont cold. Or maybe Winnipeg. God. From Washington to Montana, everything was covered with at least a foot of snow, and in some places more. But it was also a glorious time: the dinosaurs were finally tamed so things were way safer, and you could find Neanderthals riding Great Woolly Mammoths from cave dwelling to cave dwelling, spreading the day's news.

Then, tragedy struck. No one saw it coming, although cave records show Neanderthal women TOTALLY knew what was going on and kept trying to tell the men and/or their husbands but those dudes just blew them off with big, pained eye-rolls, with the head Neanderthal guy giving a (not so) sly thumb-pointing gesture to communicate "getta load a deez broads" and they all got a good chuckle out of it but the women Neanderthals were really steamed about the bad treatment and they kind of got together and talked about it and if you follow the genealogy this group of Neanderthal women are direct antecedents of Gloria Steinem.

And the pay gap was even worse back then. If you can imagine.

Anyway, what these cavewomen knew was that the Clark Fork River got plugged with some nonmeltable snow and made something called Glacial Lake Missoula. Then, that nonmeltable snow melted all at once on an unseasonably warm

July day, and Glacial Lake Missoula had grown
super big in the meantime, so the "dam" in the
Clark Fork River that made the lake in the first
place was pretty much suddenly gone.

So the water raced across Idaho, Washington, and
Oregon until it hit the Pacific Ocean. But what
you don't know is, given that Glacial Lake
Missoula spanned 3,000 square miles and reached
depths of 2,000 feet, and given the terrain, some
of the floodwaters were roughly 1,130 feet high
and traveled a robust, albeit legal, 65 miles an
hour.

These were called the Missoula Floods, and they
happened a bunch of times, and it killed the poor
newly tamed dinosaurs and wiped out the complex,
albeit sexist and potentially misogynistic Neanderthal society, thereby eliminating sexism and
misogyny forever. Thank goodness.

Oh, more importantly, in Eastern Washington these
floods not only carved out a series of mini-Grand
Canyons and left behind a chain of mini-glacial
lakes within which the State Government likes to
plant rainbow trout, but also created Sun Lakes
Resort, located at, you guessed it, Sun Lakes-Dry
Falls State Park.

Amenities include the following:

- RV park/campsites (if you're insane)
- Cabins with bathrooms and showers (if
  you're normal)
- Pool (cold)
- Mini-golf course (Putt-Putt)

- Nine-hole golf course (pretty much real)
- Water Wars (water balloon team fight course thing)
- Fishing dock (I haven't caught anything from it)
- Boat launch (I've caught plenty of trout from the boat while drinking — no, I wasn't driving)
- Paddleboards and Aqua-Cycles
- Duke's Diner (snack shack; I love snack shacks)
- Grocery store (a.k.a. beer/wine/cigarettes)

Now that's my kind of fishing.

This place is totally worth a visit. And compared to standing in the Pacific Ocean at midnight taking breakers to the face, it's a total cakewalk. I've heard that in July it turns into a party stop for 18- to 28-year-olds, with lots of weed and hard seltzers and premarital sex and drunken boating, so maybe go before then.

It's worth it, even if there's not a trout derby going on.

SUMMERTIME CYCLING DOESN'T REQUIRE CORPORATE SPONSORSHIP

SPRING 2021

May is a great time to sell a boat. Or a bicycle. At least in the Pacific Northwest.

Or buy one. Of each.

This is because we great citizens of this great region know, with certainty, that May signals the beginning of the Dry Season.

That's right, roughly 122 days of glowing warmth emanating from that giant space orb in the sky, irradiating our gentle yet ruggedly handsome faces while propagating field after field of glorious marijuana plants hidden in secret grow operations up and down the Coast — which no longer need to be secret because cannabis is legal.

That's right, haven't you heard? Cannabis is LEGAL! What's next, cocaine? Do we really want to bankrupt all those cartels? Although we might be more productive at work or during our fitness regimen with just a teeny bit of cocaine.

Indeed, it turns out all those conspiracy theorists/avid smokers I knew in college were right, and marijuana really isn't dangerous, other than the putting-it-in-your-lungs part and the fact that you can technically get too wasted off it and thus shouldn't drive a car when super stoned… or captain a boat…or ride a bike…or do some banking…although, back to the boat thing, you could just float around in a lake like Jeff Spicoli, lying in the bottom of a dinghy staring at the sky; that would be mostly safe, and super fun.

And perhaps in fact yes, the alcohol industry, combined with the cotton industry, really did quash marijuana and hemp production in the early 20th century out of a morbid fear it would be embraced by the public and render their more dangerous and/or environmentally damaging products less appealing.

Who knew? Oh yeah, Dan, Ben, Jason, Chris, and everyone else I met at the University of Washington between 1993 and 1997 who discussed theories through plumes of marijuana smoke and ended up going to law school and now either work for King County or practice corporate law at some big firm.

Sorry I doubted you.

And 122 days is actually wildly inaccurate. You have to back out the entire month of June, so it's 92. Ninety-two sunny days here in our great country, the Pacific Northwest.

Okay, that's not right either, probably like 50 sunny days in total, and 30 days where it should be sunny but something happened and it's cloudy or possibly drizzly.

And the other 12 days are where you just don't feel like doing anything because you're stoned, or perhaps you just had a few too many bong rips the night before.

(Maybe, now that's its legal, "bong rips" is less of a thing, and a more elegant vehicle for THC ingestion exists. But I'm pretty sure corporate lawyers still take bong rips.)

Speaking of bicycles, you may have heard there's a global shortage as a result of some factories shutting down for a while in 2020, coupled with exploding demand as cycling remains a great option for both staying in shape and experiencing "family fun" during the pandemic. Many bike shops went out of business, some owners determined a lack of inventory means it's a great time to retire, and other places (like the one by my house) are kind of up in the air about future plans.

So if you have a bicycle, count yourself lucky. And maybe put like 500 locks on it as bike theft is up as much as 30% in some areas. The bike shop by my house said virtually every bike they see on OfferUp is stolen, with Craigslist coming in a close second. One guy even said the photo of his stolen bike advertised on OfferUp was actually taken at his own house, moments before it was jacked.

But don't let global shortages and crime stop you from riding a bike this summer. Steal one if you must. Cycling is so great — liberating, dangerous enough that occasional spikes of adrenaline leave you completely electrified, and certainly sweat-inducing. Plus you get to see stuff that you don't get to see from a treadmill, stationary bike, or Peloton video, namely, other neighbor-hoods that are nicer than yours, other cars that are nicer than yours, other families that are nicer and better looking than yours, political signs you don't agree with, new teriyaki places, and really nice weed shops.

If you do choose to cycle this dry season, there are several people in this conference room who want to share a few fun tips and/or observations. Consider it unsolicited advice you should take under consideration and absolutely follow without complaint:

1. People driving automobiles are likely stoned. Okay, not "likely" — *are* stoned. Sure, some of them may be high from THC-laden marijuana, but ALL of them have phones, and they're fiddling with them, looking at them, getting stressed out as they hear the incessant "ping ping ping" of their absolutely vapid incoming text messages — so these fools don't see you. You don't exist. They're only thinking about their phone and mari-juana. They'll turn left in front of you,

they'll pass you and turn right in front of you, they'll pull into the intersection in front of you, etc.

This doesn't mean you shouldn't cycle. This does mean you should realize when you ride that you're running a gauntlet and you need to pay attention.

2. If you have a family or significant other, cycling is a great way to get out of the house so you don't have to talk to them. If you live alone, cycling is a great way to get away from yourself.

3. Cycling gear is ridiculous. You're not Lance Armstrong or (more contemporaneously) Wout van Aert (actual name). Therefore your skintight, wind-resistant Bahrain-McLaren or Team INEOS Competizione jersey or (much worse) pair of incredibly unforgiving Movistar bike shorts are entirely unnecessary.

That being said, people like what they like, and we appreciate that. At a minimum, however, before entering a food and beverage business post-ride, please change into some normal shorts or sweat-pants or something. There's nothing worse than witnessing you clickety-clack-clacking around in your racing shoes with your helmet on and tightly framed buns waving in everyone's face, then acting like you're the only cool person in the room. There, we said it.

4. You can't ride through crosswalks. Crosswalks are meant for walking. Otherwise they'd be called "crossrolls." If you get hit by a car riding your

bike through a crosswalk and you sue, you'll lose. We've tried.

Secondary to this, if you ride on a sidewalk and you're over the age of eight and not in a suburban area, you will crash.

5. In the metro Seattle area, cyclists can now treat stop signs as yield signs. Which is fine, if you understand what "yield" means. For example, the Revised Code of Washington (RCW 46.61.190) insists yield means slow or stop to merge with oncoming traffic. So even if you whip around the corner or seamlessly merge next to an SUV at 28 miles per hour, that may look cool, and you may be cool and coordinated, but you're still potentially sending that BMW X5 through a bakery storefront as a result of your dream of getting a Vodafone sponsorship and riding in the next Giro d'Italia.

Secondary to this, don't act all pissed when the traffic seas don't part to let you in. No one cares.

6. If you're lucky enough to have a bike trail or path near you, ride on that. Inevitably, said path will also have bipedal humanoids on it, and as irritating as it is, plan on their weaving and wobbling all over the place as they look at plants, chase their kids, argue, gossip about friends, and complain about spouses.

7. All sorts of bikes are cool these days. Cruisers with baskets, dirt bikes, road bikes, mountain bikes, hybrids, electric — so get one

and ride. The only suspect bikes currently on the market are the single-gear "fixies," whose reputation was tainted by the tens of thousands of urban-dwelling millennials who exclusively rode them from 2012 to 2018 as a way to demonstrate hipness, date-ability, and love of farmer's markets.

8. People in general are rooting for you. Cycling is all about freedom, escape, turning off the noise, enjoying the weather, stress reduction, simplicity, and the satisfaction of completing a journey. Create the space you need, be careful, and generally people will leave you alone.

So get out there and ride while the weather-getting is good — it's great. Maybe ask for a serial number or other form of history if you're buying a bike online so you know it's not "hot." And sure, maybe smoking a little weed enhances the experience if you're into that kind of thing and can handle yourself. No problem. Just don't get super stoned. And definitely avoid the cocaine.

MOTORSPORTS DIRECTLY THREATEN THE COGNITIVE BEHAVIORAL THERAPY MARKETPLACE

SPRING 2021

I used to work with a guy who always blathered on about this place called Pacific Raceways. Especially in the summer, as it turns out most motorsports in Washington State need to take place in the summer or early fall so as to avoid the sky water. Something about the coefficient of friction…and fans not wanting to get sopping wet.

We'd wrap up our day in the office (oh man, I hate offices, especially in the summer…the over-cold forced air, the energy-efficient, soundproof, tinted windows literally stripping the joy out of the sunlight, the coworkers asking you for the *millionth* time to stop rummaging through their stuff when they're away from their desks), and Paul, yes his name was Paul, would excitedly rush to go sit in Interstate 5 North's wall of immovable traffic, to basically get to Pacific

Raceways in time to watch more traffic. Albeit moving faster.

Paul was a young, robust kid, probably 25, very gregarious and helpful, which is why he made a good salesman. Very professional too, and highly adept at wearing business casual clothes. I bring this up because there's a misconception that people who watch motorsports are Lite® beer-swilling, toothless hillbillies with one foot on the stoop, another on the hound dog, a double barrel shotgun over their shoulder, and a giant wooden mixing paddle grasped in both hands, gently swirling dat pot'a moonshine dey're a boilin' up on the front porch fer grandma as they lean over dem vapors just a bit ta catch a buzz and getter better glimpse o' dat ol' TV dat's a playin' da Car Razin' games…

Oh man, I'm so sorry. That's really offensive. I don't know what got into me. I think what happened is…well, whether professional or hill-billy, I'm starting to see the allure of motor-sport watchin'…er, watching motorsports. I'm going to have to tell my therapist about this.

Watching humans encased in metal whipping them-selves around in circles, figure eights, squiggly lines, or even one long, straight line (if you're into NHRA — an acronym for the nonfictional National Hot Rod Association, a.k.a. "Funny Car" racing) at ludicrous speeds all comes down to one thing, and that one thing is The Overlooked Problem In Our Society That We Can't Ever Do Anything About.

Yes, there's a big problem our society refuses to address, clearly avoids, and routinely, likely daily, sweeps under the rug: boys turning 16. And, in fact, girls turning 16 as well.

The unfortunate reality of human beings turning 16 in Washington, Oregon, and likely the other 48 states (excluding Alaska because there are no roads there) is the fact that they can test for, apply, and receive a legal driver's license. Or an illegal one, if they choose to visit a specific Craigslist page wherein they can receive a very official-looking Russian driver's license seemingly issued by a subdivision of the General Administration for Traffic Safety of the Ministry of Internal Affairs, but which in reality comes from my very fancy card printer in my basement yet proves effective for remedying traffic violations/infractions when coupled with Russian diplomatic license plates, which I also may or may not have access to, for a very reasonable price.

I don't really know what modern 16-year-olds are interested in because I'm afraid of them. Frankly, I don't want to know. But if they're anything like the 16-year-old me, they're interested in getting away from their parents once in a while through the freedom offered by motorized vehicles, electric or otherwise, with a wheel count ranging from two to four, in general.

(Speaking of vehicles, I recently read that those electronic charging stations or "charge points," the most conspicuous of which go by clever but entirely confusing names like "chargepoin+," "EVgo," or "TESLA Supercharging Stations," actually utilize tiny but efficient fossil fuel-powered internal combustion engines to generate electricity, which seems to defeat the purpose of having an electric vehicle but explains the smoke emanating from the exhaust pipe located on top of the charging unit, as well as the double-trailered oil tanker trucks constantly parked next to them. At least by my house.)

Indeed, regardless of the hypocrisy, young people with newly acquired driver's licenses likely want to get out there and determine exactly how violently they can turn without rolling over, as well as how fast they can go without getting arrested. This has to be the case because that's what I did. And the answer to your question is "never convicted."

Here's just a brief examination of how I expressed my newfound freedom at that time, a freedom I wish I had now, what with having a wife, kid, dog, mortgage, tax liabilities, and a boss I frequently inspire to suffer from nervous breakdowns.

At approximately 16.5 years old and legal to drive, I hopped into my parents' 1984 Volkswagen Quantum (brown, four-door, front-wheel-drive, with straight five cylinders of what seemed like awesome power) and promptly

- picked up my unlicensed friend Jon, drove to the church parking lot by his house,

which was conveniently free of wheel stops
(those little mini-curbs at the end of
parking spaces), and just absolutely mashed
the accelerator down, alternatingly
cranking the wheel right and/or left in a
haphazard fashion as he just kept saying
"dude, dude, DUDE" over and over again
whilst grasping the roof handle/grab
handle/panic handle thing

- later, picked up my newly licensed friend
  Jon or Jeff, depending on availability, and
  found a convenient, incredibly long,
  incredibly straight gravity hill (downhill
  slope followed by an uphill slope) on
  Highway 16 near Gig Harbor, where, if the
  wind blew out of the east and I mashed the
  accelerator down again, that 1984
  Volkswagen Quantum could achieve a top
  speed of 122 miles per hour

- when it was raining, picked up my newly
  licensed friend Jon or Jeff, depending on
  availability (this time in my parent's
  behemoth rear-wheel-drive Cadillac), and
  utilized my expert knowledge of physics,
  particularly gravity (again...gravity is a
  big deal when you're 16) as it relates to
  the previously mentioned coefficient of
  friction, to align said Cadillac at the
  bottom of Carr Street hill (mammoth of a
  hill, at least two city blocks long) in
  such a way that it pointed to the top, then
  mashed the accelerator down so the Cadillac
  fishtailed or, as I liked to think, "did a
  burnout" all the way up the hill

- routinely found any piles of gravel, anywhere, in any kind of vehicle, and did a bunch of burnouts
- tried to burn out anywhere else, wherever possible
- consistently did not get dates

So the truth of the matter is, motorsports exist because all humans turn 16 and subsequently want to race cars, and motorcycles too if they're available. Then, at a certain point in their lives, possibly in response to what may have been a violation of a municipal code, or state or federal "law," they realize this is a bad idea and they'd better "straighten up and fly right" if they want to continue to live (and eat) for free at their parents' house.

But that hankering for speed, g-forces, burnt rubber, and fishtailing madness never goes away. For any of us. Think about it…what do you drive? Let me guess, it's some form of family-friendly sedan, SUV, hybrid, or (oh I'm so sorry) MINIVAN. But do you know what your real problem is? ALL-WHEEL DRIVE. It's hard enough to do burnouts with your fancy airbag collision alert heads-up display blind spot alarms going off all the time… but with ALL-WHEEL DRIVE, it's impossible.

It's just not going to happen. And it's probably for the best. You have kids or, if not, kids in your neighborhood. And now you're a boring, responsible adult. You think about insurance premiums and wear-and-tear on tires. You don't want to go to jail. You eat chicken breast

without the skin and avocados — not because
avocados taste good, but because you heard
they're good for "heart health."

It's all okay. Because you have Pacific Raceways:

- A 2.25-mile road course with nine turns
  racing stock cars, "screaming Ultra Super
  Bikes," historical sports cars, 150-mile-
  per-hour karts, and car club vehicles
  (think Porsche enthusiasts, a.k.a. people
  worthy of punching)
- A huge grandstand, with concessions, which
  happens to be one of my favorite words
- A quarter-mile drag strip, which runs the
  previously mentioned NHRA Funny Cars, plus
  other cool vehicles, many of which also
  require parachutes to stop
- ProFormance Racing School — the first
  professional and fully accredited high
  performance and competition driving school
  in Puget Sound. Where you can learn to
  race, or (even better) enroll in their
  advanced street survival driving skill
  course
- "Lapping Days," a.k.a. High-Performance
  Sport Driving Days, on select weekends
  where [novice or seasoned] racers can tool
  around the track (they group you by
  ability) and receive instruction (classroom
  and in-car)

And if Pacific Raceways is unavailable to you
because you live in some weird place like New

Hampshire, just look around. There's a similar facility somewhere. Guaranteed.*

*not guaranteed

Just think: You could take your overcomputerized, family-friendly sedan and really let off some steam while succumbing to the urge to achieve some kind of terminal velocity, without it being a terminal event. Or maybe just watch the insanity of professional drivers breaking the sound barrier with fire shooting out of the 22 chrome tailpipes inserted all over their ridiculous vehicles. Wait. Maybe I should do all of the above. I could fire my therapist.

See you at the track.

DON'T OVERLOOK THE MARKETING CAPACITY OF PLAYOFF HOCKEY

SPRING 2021

The Stanley Cup playoffs are underway. I can tell because my friend who is a Penguins fan made me come over and watch the third period of last Saturday's game before we took our kids on a somewhat death-defying bike ride. I can also tell because the five other people in Seattle who follow NHL hockey were home watching the game that day, judging by the 624,300 riders we later encountered on the Burke Gilman trail, indicating everyone was out and about in the good weather. The remaining 100,000 citizens apparently congregated at all of our other predesignated stops, including Gas Works Park, Lake Union (in various watercraft), and every brewery in Ballard where we therefore could not get in to drink beer. Well, my friend and I at least. The kids were going to have to fend for themselves.

Okay, obviously there is, in theory, a large population of hockey fans here in Seattle; otherwise the whole "It's the Seattle Kraken" or whatever the forthcoming professional hockey team is called wouldn't be forthcoming, nor would the $930-million Climate Pledge Arena. And the newly constant, spontaneous outbreaks of fistfights in the streets — complete with "Jerseying" (the act of reaching over somebody and pulling their shirt over their heads, but not off, so their arms are not usable for fighting or defending themselves, and their eyes are not usable for seeing), ripping off of sunglasses and hats, snatching of wallets and tossing them into the street, and other general mayhem — lo, that would not be happening either.

As I watched the Pittsburgh Penguins battle the Staten Island Islanders, or whatever deeply considered name that team has, I marveled at the incredible speed and hand-eye coordination of the players (the other night some guy on the Penguins tapped a puck into the goal with the teeniest part of his stick, just below the handle, as it sailed toward him at 133 m.p.h.), as well as their long, greasy "party in the back" haircuts. Their visible desire to impart sheer, wanton, cruel physical violence onto virtually anything (including the ice, the wall, and the frame that holds the net on the goal) was also really impressive. I imagine Uber bans hockey players from their ride-sharing service out of fear that a given player will just hop in the back and start smashing things out of habit.

There is a stark contrast amongst these folks, though — I'm not sure how one develops the blood-lust, cruelty, and physicality of a Tasmanian devil (at least the cartoon kind) while culti-vating the ability to skate with such elegance it makes a grown man weep (or so I hear), but what-ever Saskatchewan-based forced labor camps these guys are sent to at birth certainly have the training regimen down. It's probably taken from the playbooks of the Bollettieri Tennis Academy, the training center for the Russian National Olympic Gymnastics Team, or any parochial school.

I will say, as a seven-time visitor to Angel of the Winds Arena in Everett, home of the appropri-ately violent Everett Silvertips, hockey is super fun to watch in real life. Which is why you should pick me up as soon as we can all go back to sporting events, take me to Angel of the Winds Arena, buy me a ticket, give me some cash for snacks, leave, and wait in the parking lot for me to text that I'm ready to be picked up when the game is over.

The Everett Silvertips are a major junior ice hockey team and current members of the U.S. Divi-sion in the Western Conference of the Western Hockey League (WHL). The WHL itself is based in Western Canada (Canadians are really into hockey, Molson Canadian, and being weirdly nice) and the Northwestern United States. It's one of three leagues that constitute the Canadian Hockey League as the highest level of junior hockey in Russia. I mean Canada.

Players are basically 15- to 20-year-old ex-convicts on work release. It's like in *The Running Man*: their crimes have been fabricated, and their only way out is to make it to the NHL. So they're super motivated, as evidenced by their frenetic punching of each other at any given moment.

Outside of Everett, if you live in one of the following areas, you can watch your local WHL team in action:

- Portland (Winterhawks)
- Seattle (Thunderbirds)
- Spokane (Chiefs)
- Tri-City (Americans) — although we all know the tri-cities don't exist

The rink (at least in Everett) offers an intimacy hard to come by in other professional sports. No matter how cheap your seat is, you can almost feel the reverberations as players ricochet off the plexiglass, and I have yet to have a bad view of the ice. Plus there's all sorts of family-fun hijinks for the crowd to enjoy, many of which are now my all-time favorites:

T-shirt bazooka — Dude walks around pointing a 60-millimeter, air-powered, tubular, nonlethal rocket launcher at whichever section screams the loudest, and people just go nuts trying to get him to pull the trigger and receive that precious, Chinese chemical—smelling piece of T-shirt schwag, despite a 90% chance it won't fit.

This joyful weapon also makes a satisfying *"wump"* with each discharge.

T-shirt cannon — Local car dealership's nicest Ford F-150, completely emblazoned with said dealership's logos, trolls around the rink with dude in back pointing this truck bed-mounted, T-shirt-shooting version of a TOW Anti-Tank Missile at various desperately screaming sections of fans, resulting in the same outcome as above, but with a much louder *"wump."*

***The Everett Hindenburg* (actual name) remote-controlled blimp** — Strangely, this minidirigible is filled with explosive hydrogen gas à la its namesake, despite the protests of and pending legal action by the Snohomish County Department of Emergency Management. Nonetheless, it appears at least twice a game, releasing toy surprises from one of the eight or so also-remote-controlled-which-is-cool clips fastened to its underside, much to the delight of the howling, salivating crowd, regardless of their age.

Chuck-a-puck — This one I think you have to pay for, I can't quite remember. But basically let's say Angel of the Winds Arena holds about 10,000 fans. Roughly 6,000 of those fans, including me, buy one or more of these soft, rubberish pucks with a number on them. Then, during one of the 18-minute intermissions, everyone throws their puck at a series of tires lined up in the middle of the arena. The closer you get to the tires, the more likely you are to win a prize. Even if you don't win (I never have, to the point where I question the actual existence of these "prizes"), it's great fun to watch pucks land in people-with-the-rinkside-seats' nachos, beers, and Dippin' Dots, coupled with an occasional bounce off the noggin'.

Some other hijinks — At some point during another intermission, you may be delighted by a relay race with humans battling each other over inconsequential trinkets while falling all over the place, some lady trying to score a goal from center ice for a prize, and sometimes a cute dog race, although I may have imagined the last event based on consuming copious amounts of Molson Canadian.

Also, throughout the game the local Ford dealership parades that F-150 across the ice like a 17th-century landowner looking for an aristocratic suitor for his daughter, even during the briefest pauses in play, to the point where I've seen a last-second shot on goal actually bounce off the rear driver's-side tire, much to the chagrin of Silvertips forward Hunter Campbell, but obviously that dealership is trying to squeeze every drop out of the promotional dollars invested from whatever (likely cash-only) shady arrangement they made with the team, and with Angel of the Winds Arena.

But it's all good family fun. Even if you don't like violent sports, a hockey game is worth checking out, especially when you're watching young kids trying to go pro, which virtually every WHL player is trying to do. I admire their drive and moxie — it inspires me to also try and do great things, even something simple like buying a new truck.

IF YOU START TRAINING NOW, YOU'LL BE READY BY JULY 25TH

SPRING 2021

The annual Seattle summer celebration known as Seafair, with its boat races, partying, and general bedlam, is tomorrow, and you should get ready.

What? Oh, it's not actually tomorrow. Oops! Sorry about that. Apparently it's still 12 weeks away. Well, the main weekend event with the boat races is 12 weeks away (August 5th). If you consider the fact that Seafair also bought the rights to the Seattle version of the Fourth of July, renaming it "Seafair Summer Fourth," it's more like 7 weeks away.

We didn't realize federal holidays were available for retail purchase.

The point is, Seafair was cancelled last year, and since we haven't left the house before, during, or after that time, we jumped the gun a bit with this announcement, in anticipation of having something to talk about. In fact, we're antsy to do anything besides look at our front yard, within which the little neighborhood 11-year-olds established a fiefdom, completely inde-pendent of our influence, essentially sovereign, as communicated by the Nerf darts they rain down on us as we try to make a run to the store.

Oh boy, there's a lot to it. Seafair, that is. A Torchlight Run. Milk Carton Derby. Torchlight Parade. A Bunch of Other Stuff. Then the Arc de Triomphe — the hydroplane* races coupled with an air show courtesy of the Blue Angels.

*Hydroplanes are really fast boats propelled by airplane jet engines. No joke.

Oh! We just received a letter via speedy courier. It turns out we have to be official about this story, and officially speaking, Seafair events are spoken or written of in the following manner:

- Seafair Summer Fourth — Presented By Homestreet Bank
- Torchlight Run — Presented by Capital One Café
- Seafair Milk Carton Derby (surprisingly lacking loud sponsorship)
- Alaska Airlines Torchlight Parade
- Seafair Weekend Festival featuring the Boeing Seafair Air Show and Homestreet Bank Cup (with the hydroplanes/jet boats… formerly known as the Seafair Cup)

Sheesh. Come on, you guys, this is just too difficult. If you want people to include your various sponsorship entities within the spoken titles of your event, you need to come up with better names. Something within the vernacular or something. We know it's hard, but you seem like bright people so surely you can come up with something.

Of these events, we've witnessed only two:

- The Torchlight Parade, which we were forced to endure thanks to employment at a coffee shop located along the parade route. It was crazy. People started setting up their chairs at like 10 a.m. We assume they didn't have jobs. Although they definitely came in to buy stuff. Or use the bathroom. Technically our shift wrapped up well before it actually got dark — the dark being a key ingredient in making a good Torchlight Parade — so while we haven't actually seen the procession in action, we feel like we still experienced its spirit, as well as a lot of tank tops, several of which seamlessly incorporated an image of the American flag. Plus whatever you're thinking in your head right now is pretty much what the parade probably looks like, and if you take that and add the sweet, greasy aroma of funnel cakes, boom, it's like you're magically there.

Okay fine, maybe that doesn't count. Scratch it off the list.

- Nothing else. Oops. How un-communitarian and by proxy un-corporately supportive of us. This list is a disaster.

You are likely shocked, and wondering how we have lived in the general Puget Sound area for 87 years and not participated in the Seafair Weekend Festival, which involves making a trip to Lake Washington with a boat to tie off on a gigantic log boom that consists of murdered trees and spending all weekend (we think you have to set up on Thursday to get a good spot, so really it's like four days, and we also assume these partici-pants don't have jobs) watching professional lunatics fly their buoyant jet planes across the water, occasionally (and much to the delight of the unemployed crowd) actually disconnecting from the lake and flying up and off through the air in somersaults, while the United States Navy Marketing Machine routinely violates the City of Seattle's Noise Ordinance, as established and enforced by the Seattle Department of Construc-tion and Inspections (SDCI) with a squadron of F/A-18 fighter/bombers.

It's because we don't like being touched.

A peer of ours who regularly ties off at the log boom every Thursday prior to the event only to wake up the following Monday afternoon adrift in a sea of empty raspberry White Claw cans and the occasional body just can't get enough of this thing and describes (to his delight and our horror) how great it is this way: "You spend the day drinking and people just crawl across all the boats tied off to each other all day and they just end up in your boat and it's one big party."

No thanks. The last thing we want is for some potbellied, red- tanned attorney in an American-flag (there it is again) pair of (hopefully knee-length) swim trunks slapping us on the back with his sweaty hand as his big-boobed, bikini-topped, and torn-jean-short-wearing wife shoves past us asking if we have any vodka and some sunscreen while slurring how she "needs to find a spot to pee."

Nope. No thank you. You're violating our personal space for real. No touching and transference of your ample body sweat, please and thank you.

But there is a super secret part of Seattle's annual Seafair tradition worth devoting your time, personal space, and body sweat to: the Seafair Triathlon (currently available for overt corporate sponsorship — a good fit for a "Brought to You by McDonald's; Try Our Spicy Chicken Nuggets with Mighty Hot Sauce" tagline…or maybe just "McDonald's; Eat Our McPlant," which turns out to be an actual menu item).

We love triathletes because, while they are, like most fitness enthusiasts, insane, triathloning by its very nature doesn't involve lots of personal contact or unnecessary conversation. In fact, it's a fairly isolating sport, as participants need to train

- in the pool, which is virtually impossible to sweat or conversate in, and since now that we think about it we humans do likely sweat in the water, at least what sweat comes out is annihilated by copious amounts of chlorine
- in the open water — you can't just train in the pool, because then you'll be woefully unprepared for open water swimming, which features waves hitting your face while you're trying to breathe and vast populations of frightening little sea creatures rollicking about, as evidenced by that time we saw a muskrat or some other evil being in the shallows of the lake we were training in and absolutely freaked out
- on a bicycle, which requires complete immersion as otherwise it's easy to get hit by a truck
- on feet, as in running, which leads to breathlessness (no conversation!) and results in such sheer misery that, even if running in a group, all you can really do is grimace at each other

The best part about the Seafair Triathlon is its overall ease of use, relatively speaking. Meaning, you get to pick from the least intimidating kinds of triathlon races: Super Sprint, Sprint, Duathlon, Relay, or (if you're a kid) the Kids Triathlon. The latter of which, it turns out, requires you to actually be under 12 or something in order to participate. We tried, but as we towered above the other racers we were yanked out of the start and reprimanded.

The key here is having the Super Sprint and Sprint options to choose from. We don't know anything about Duathlons or Relays, but since the names imply other people are involved, a.k.a. teammates one would have to speak and possibly hang out with, we caution against them. Basically this means you get to pick from the following:

- Super Sprint: Swim .3 miles, bike 6.2 miles, run 1.6 miles (one after the other; they discourage breaks, as we discovered). Training required: 3-4 hours per week
- Sprint: Swim .46 miles, bike 12.4 miles, run 3.1 miles. Training required: 3-5 hours per week. We don't know what the extra hour is for. Perhaps reflecting on your life's regrets.

This is all way better than the other generally accepted triathlon distance options, which include the following swim/bike/run mileage ratios: Olympic (1/25/62), Half (1.2/56/13) and Full (2.4/112/26.2 plus an approximately 12- to 15-mile transport to the emergency room).

Additionally, if you choose to do a triathlon, you pretty much have to train if you want to actually finish, and being gone for at least 60 consecutive minutes, five days a week, really puts you in a great position to not be bothered by other people. If you choose to participate in some nerd triathlon training group, the bet's off though, so you only have yourself to blame when that dude starts talking about how his V.P. of Sales is an idiot and if only he could get the right pricing he'd be able to really kill it, etc., etc. Or God forbid some other work story that reflects how we all have problems with our professional peers. And don't even get us started on stories revolving around having trouble with Millennials, Gen Z, and all the other stuff that never changes but in fact is just a symptom of getting old.

Additionally, you get to buy or steal a bike, a nose plug if you're like us and just so sensitive that chlorine really bugs you, and a new pair of running shoes that can easily double as your Going-out-to-Dinner Shoes, despite what your partner says.

Finally, you'll get super fit. It's inevitable. Unless you offset all the calories burned by eating Spicy Chicken Nuggets with Mighty Hot Sauce every day. But who does that?

And there is that sense of accomplishment — not so much from the race, but from the training. When you practice an intense swim, then instantly hop on a bike and crank away, then drop that bike and run for a few miles, you start to feel like you can do anything.

Or so we hear.

This year's Seafair Triathlon is July 25th. See you there. Watch out for the muskrats.

SPORTS FANS AND CULINARY ENTHUSIASTS ARE ONE AND THE SAME

ALMOST SUMMER 2021

The most important part of professional sports is the food. In fact, anthropological studies indicate that throughout human history, the progression of different ingredient combinations to create a given meal directly relates to our universal desire to ingest something delicious while watching someone else compete.

It's kind of a parasympathetic nervous system/psychological situation where we empathize with the loss of calories the competitor experiences, so our brain stem tells our hands to dip the Fritos in the Cheez Dip, then maybe some Five-Alarm Chili, and wash it all down with an ice-cold beer, like a nice clean, crisp pilsner. Mmmmmmmm, God we love icy cold beer.

Like most things in life, it all traces back to our caveman ancestors: Approximately 15,000 years ago, Glorb, Ignot, and Zrrg sat in their cave entrance munching on Flintstones-sized chicken legs, watching poor (but fast) Ungr run like hell back to the cave, with the day's berry harvest in a banana-leaf woven basket and an enraged saber-toothed tiger hot on his tail, snarling, thick sputum covering its hungry, horrible face. And the beast, mad with hunger, steadily gains ground, five yards for every yard earned by Ungr, and the tension builds, now Ungr can feel the creature's hot breath on the back of his legs it's so close, hear the thud of each huge paw striking the earth, tearing at the soft clay in its desperation to reach and devour, and Glorb, Ignot, and Zrrg don't really want Ungr to get eaten but damn isn't this fun to watch and can you pass the chips?

Thus the birth of competitive sports-watching, and the culinary delights behind it.

You may be

- sitting around for roughly seven months rewatching old Super Bowls as you wait for the NFL season to start (and occasionally checking out nfl.com, which only serves as a placeholder for boring stories about intra- and inter-league drama during the offseason, coupled with completely ridiculous "way too early" predictions for the upcoming season, which the writers/contributors are likely happy to produce just to stay employed since absolutely nothing is going on)

- watching a weekly bocce ball game at a park
  where the court/empty patch of grass is
  covered in goose droppings and cigarette
  butts and the old guys playing may be in
  the Mafia but it's hard to tell and you
  kind of hope they are
- actually at a venue…let's see here, like
  Moda Center — which, as of this writing, is
  empty because the Portland Trail Blazers
  were in that whole "win or go home"
  situation and they lost so now they're
  home, sitting around, sad, in their
  mansions. Which are pretty good places to
  be sad in, especially considering their
  private chefs are probably serving them all
  the stuff they couldn't eat during the
  regular season, like Beef Wellington* and
  foie gras**

*Beef Wellington is beef tenderloin or filet
mignon coated with pâte and duxelles (mushrooms
and herbs sauteed in butter), wrapped in puff
pastry, then baked. It's like a corn dog for rich
people.

**Nobody knows what foie gras is.

Whatever you're watching, your hypothalamus is
telling you sports equals food, and food equals
sports, so dive into some sports-related foodstuffs. Don't fret about it. Swimsuit season is
overrated. And you're probably married or otherwise in some form of tense, weird, way too heavy,
but-I-thought-it-was-a-fling relationship, so
feel free to really let yourself go.

Just don't look online for your game-time meal inspiration. Other than right here at Oregon Sports News, of course; online right here is a nice, warm, cuddly, safe, empathetic place that frequently compliments your shoes. Everywhere else online is enraging.

Case in point: We received a federal grant for $650,000 and convened a group of scientists from the University of Oregon and Oregon State to produce a study to determine what happens when a 25- to 45-year-old metropolitan-dwelling, professional, really attractive female, who's okay with married guys…oh wait, sorry, that was for something else. This study was to determine what happens when sports fans type "Best Foods to Watch Sports" into a Google search bar. Or possibly a DuckDuckGo search bar.

Also, the University of Oregon and Oregon State scientists just ended up smoking cannabis the whole time and talking about John Muir, so we had to kick them out and hire scientists from the University of Washington and Washington State. Which was only marginally better, as these folks also smoked lots of cannabis and just droned on and on about socialism. So we found scientists from Renton Technical College and an online forum in Eastern Europe; these folks were great. It turns out the future of education lies with technical schools and online education platforms.

The results of the study, whose budget quickly ballooned to $1.1 million, are as follows, according to the final report:

When people type "Best foods for watching sports" into a Google or other listing site's search bar, no matter how cute and appealing this other listing site's social mission is, we, the Scientists of Greater Renton and Greater Albania Online, conclude that the following happens:

1. A series of unhelpful, SEO-friendly stories appear, as evidenced by "Fifteen Foods For Tailgating and Watching Sports," published by The Good Men Project. Top menu items include chili — "a cold-weather favorite" — guacamole, and chicken wings.

As scientists we won't even bother testing our hypothesis that literally every sports fan in America already understands chili, guacamole, and chicken wings are fun to eat while watching sports, fun to eat in the middle of the night, fun to eat at a picnic, fun to eat while signing a mortgage agree-ment, fun to eat when finding out you're getting a divorce, and fun to eat in general, making this information redundant at best.

2. Frequently, past search inquiries made by the general public pop up, the most prom-inent of which is "What should I eat while watching football?"

As scientists who benefit from the large

federal grants produced in the United States, we'd like to officially go on record stating this kind of phraseology is a threat to National Security.

First, if U.S. citizens are truly asking a cold, dead, computer algorithm what to eat before watching what amounts to the United States Constitution in action because they're so worried that if they don't curate the absolutely perfect "dish," the experience won't be maximized and they won't have content to publish on Instagram, you might as well just hand over your great country back to England and be all like, "We tried. It's too hard."

Second, this frequent past search inquiry only yields more SEO-friendly information/menu items from banal articles in the liberty-stealing, autocrat-inspiring, Stalinist digital and print magazine/anarchist rag *Men's Health*, as evidenced by their suggestion that the best foods for watching sports are

- grilled hot dogs
- beer nuts
- pizza bagel bites
- massive meatballs
- peach and Brie quesadillas

Peach and Brie quesadillas may sound good to the THC-infused, munchie-afflicted scientist at the University of Oregon, Oregon State University, the University of Washington, and Washington State University, but we here in the real scientific community can prove they are truly gross. And, not unlike The Good Men Project's results, the rest of the list is obvious, unhelpful, and redundant.

Do you have any more grant money? Thank you.

-The Scientists

So the big takeaway is to not conduct general online searches for deliciousness as they only yield demand generation marketing tactics by communist organizations. Instead pick one of the following well-researched, delicious things to eat while watching tennis, golf, baseball, playoff basketball, or playoff hockey. There may be other sports going on right now, we're not sure, but you get the idea:

- The donut burger — juicy burger patty served in the middle of a glazed donut, topped with American cheese, crispy applewood-smoked bacon, and spicy cherry pepper jam
- Asada dog — 18-inch, grass-fed beef hot dog tucked into a telera roll — similar to a French roll — with fries, queso blanco, salsa, the appropriate use of guacamole, and carne asada for double meatiness
- Fat's chicken sandwich — five-spice fried

chicken thigh on a perfectly dense bun
served with poutine, mac and cheese, and
rice topped with andouille sausage gravy
- Any kind of lobster roll
- S'mores bacon on a stick — perfectly fried
  bacon dunked in chocolate and rolled in a
  crushed graham cracker and marshmallow
  mixture

Obviously it's easier to find this stuff at a
major sports venue, which we gratefully can now
start attending. In the meantime, we're not sure
how to make any of this at home, but you seem
like both a culinary enthusiast and a bright
person, so we're confident you can figure it out.

SPORTS BARS ARE KEY TO OUR FUTURE

SUMMER 2021, MERCIFULLY SO

Aside from being great places to watch sports, drink beer, hide from spouses, kids, and other mundane obligations then eventually, at the last possible moment, call an Uber to go home, sports bars are great places to become unreasonably competitive while flaunting unique skill sets like dart throwing, SkeeBall rolling, table shuffleboard puck sliding, and loud, violent Golden Tee trackball spinning.

The same can be said of local fraternities, but eventually one is deemed too old and creepy and "out of place," repeatedly kicked out, eventually denied entry, and ultimately banned from campus entirely.

Several yellowed, cracked, and ancient documents buried deep within the bowels of the National Archives and Records Administration confirm that the progenitor of all sports bars opened in Long Beach, California, in 1979, the brainchild of former L.A. Rams offensive lineman Dennis Harrah and a teeny-tiny little nine-year-old Snoop Dogg. Originally called "Real Sticky Icky," Harrah leveraged his 51% stake (Snoop only scanned the partnership agreement, reading his 49% ownership as "499%," thanks to copious amounts of marijuana smoke clouding his vision) to select the more appropriate, sports-related name of "Legends," thereby saving the sports bar genre from obscurity and securing the world a future filled with 1,279 Buffalo Wild Wings locations and, more regionally specific, one McGillacuddy's Sports Bar & Grill in Portland and one Sluggers next to T-Mobile Park in Seattle.

Legends Sports Bar created an environment where patrons could enjoy various sports broadcasts while surrounded by one of the largest private collections of sports memorabilia — from autographed baseballs by the likes of Ted Williams to Muhammad Ali's signed gloves — allowing them to temporarily forget their various crushing responsibilities, including constantly guessing what their significant other is actually saying, looking busy at work, keeping up with various Joneses, and maintaining the new sports car purchased to offset the lameness of the sensible minivan.

Of course, the sports bar genre has evolved quite a bit since then. Which you know, as you're likely sitting at one right now, possibly having a lunch featuring wings and curly fries, watching your phone repeatedly glow and vibrate as you ignore call after frantic call from your project manager, who's wondering where the deliverable is. It's fine. Just tell them, "Relax, it takes as long as it takes," then invite them over for a wing and a beer. Well, maybe a Diet Coke. You are at work.

Modern sports bars run the gamut of concepts, from super fancy to super smutty to super gimmicky to super dive-y, and everything in between. But what makes a sports bar great is not the availability of those Wagyu beef burgers, Hooters girls, bartenders in referee jerseys, or cracked leather stools and dirty bathrooms, respectively. No, it's the ready availability of those mindless games that provide a stage for us humans to demonstrate mastery — i.e., our confidence, capability, and overall talent — in order to successfully win a mate (or keep the mate we have), regardless of everyone's gender identity or sexual orientation.

Which, for example, is accomplished by throwing a 6-by-6-inch double-seamed fabric bag filled with 16 ounces of corn kernels through a 6-inch hole centered 9 inches from the top of a raised 2-by-4-foot angled wooden platform approximately 33 feet away, a.k.a. the unfortunately-but-originally-it-made-sense-named field/bar/lawn game "cornhole."

Cornhole is a courtship ritual, a mating call, and a display of ability and thus virility, designed to successfully spawn hundreds of

offspring and simultaneously suggest a willing-
ness to take care of them unless something more
interesting pops up, like an invitation from some
friends to go to a sports bar and play more
games, which obviously continues this cycle of
life and (thankfully) propagates our species.

Obviously cornhole isn't the only cool, procre-
ation-inspiring sports bar game available to the
American and European public. In fact, there's
lots of awesome games worth getting really good
at to show overall mental and physical prowess
and thereby claim a coupling partner (or further
impress an existing one, especially from some
long crazy relationship like marriage where it
just goes on and on and on and they're so used to
constant bodily noises and a preference for
walking around in threadbare underwear that it's
hard to remind them that, underneath the sloven-
liness, a real avant-garde, charming, sophisti-
cated, risk-handling, cool, nonchalant but still
caring and able-to-make-babies-type person
exists. Like Maverick from *Top Gun*).

In fact, extensive, slightly buzzed research
shows the following sports bar games (in addition
to the ones previously listed) are cool and lead
to widespread, frenetic copulating, thereby
increasing regional birth rates by as much as
44.5 per 1,000 inhabitants of places with sports
bars:

- Duffleboard (table-top mix of shuffleboard
  and mini-golf)
- Mini-Golf (a.k.a. Putt-Putt)

- Pinball (enough said, it's 'cause of The Who)
- Pool (nothing displays slick, overconfident smugness and subsequent baby-making ability like winning at pool)
- Ping-Pong, as well as Foosball (speaking to the latter, no other bar sport provides for such absolute, merciless, public humiliation of opponents)
- Axe Throwing (which is an ill-advised but increasingly popular activity nowadays)

Of course, there are some dud sports bar games. Nothing discourages rampant, passionate sex more than these:

- Karaoke
- Checkers
- Dance Dance Revolution
- Chess
- Big Ol' Coin-Op Arcade Games (excluding Golden Tee)
- "How Many Free Drinks Can We Get from the Losers Watching Sports?" (played exclusively by girls)

In fact, studies reveal these dud games decrease birth rates within the continental United States by 79%. The only thing more effective at shutting down human procreative biology is hanging out with friends who just had a baby, due to the screaming, crying, and pooping. By the baby.

So there you have it. Go flaunt your stuff at the local sports bar and get with the getting on of gaming. It's an important part of our natural world, an important mating ritual, not unlike male peacocks unfolding their glorious feathers or female praying mantises using pheromones to lure in the dopey guy mantises, then biting off their heads and eating them. Which, come to think of it, sounds a lot like the "Free Drinks" game.

Either way, get on out there. Our species is counting on you.

WE CAN'T ALL BE CAELEB DRESSEL, BUT WE CAN ALL USE A TRAMPOLINE

SUMMER 2021

The Summer Olympics are waiting like a stalking butler for most Americans to come home from work and not care. This is likely because most Americans are not true patriots, as evidenced by their proclivity to watch other, more interesting but way less jingoistic sports, like soccer.

…Wait a second here, that can't be right, can it? Ah, never mind…

Let's just agree our citizenry is more likely to watch PGA Tour golf, or the World Series of Poker, than the Summer Olympics. Unless they're over 75, in which case they're asleep in front of the Games right now. Or at least the Trials; we're a tad early.

Those poor Summer Olympic athletes. It's an all-or-nothing deal: they're either a Men's 100-Meter

Fly Gold Medal Winner with a soon-to-be-inked Wheaties endorsement, or a Women's All-Around or Vault Gold Medal Winner with a soon-to-be-inked Gatorade endorsement, or nothing — and thus going back after the Games to something useless like teaching kindergarten.

And those are the famous events with the big names and the glitter and spotlights surrounding them, like Men's 100-Meter Fly Gold Medal Contender…ah…hold on…let's look this up…Caeleb Dressel! Sheesh, take a gander at that guy's physique! Actually don't look, you'll become depressed and want to stop eating nachos. Or, if married in any form to a dude, to divorce your husband. On second thought, go ahead and sneak a peek regardless of how you identify, the only peril being you might have a heart attack thanks to Caeleb-with-two-e's' bod.

But stop thinking about Caeleb for just a second and consider the more obscure events that get no play and are only good for canoe endorsements, like the aptly named "Canoe Slalom," as excerpted from *Olympic Canoe Digest* magazine, which may or may not be real:

> Unlike the Canoe Sprint, in which competi-
> tors race on a straight, flat course, pants-
> less, which television viewers can't tell
> due to the competitors' undercarriages being
> hidden by the canoe and the networks taking
> only low-angle shots of the race but from
> the stands fans see a bunch of nether
> regions, the Canoe Slalom involves river

rapids pumped directly from the Colorado River and a series of marked gates through which paddlers must navigate without a collision or going "wheeeeeeeee!" (both incur time penalties). The sport has report- edly been a thrilling part of the games for perverts and 12 normal people since 1972.

It turns out Canoe Slalom is a thing for women too, but they wear pants, as they should, because it's been well documented they get paid less than the dudes — amongst other societal inequalities — and they just don't need to put up with any more hassle than they already do simply by being women.

Oh! Another nerd — ah, we mean obscure — event is race walking, where it's basically running except one foot is always on the ground, which results in a funky, uncomfortable-to-watch hip wiggle. From the perspective of the toilet or eating lunch alone (again) and succumbing to the warm, loving, inhuman embrace of an iPhone's blue screen, race walking looks easy, but then so do tax preparation, sherpa-ing, and building a fence, so whatever. Check it out:

- Athletes must keep one foot in contact with the ground at all times, as visible to the human eye. Judges are present at events to ensure the rule is enforced.
- If there is no visible contact, it is deemed "lifting" and attracts a penalty.
- "Your eye can catch anything that is slower

than 0.6 seconds, so the quickest lifter is going to be okay within the rules. You have to push the envelope, you want to be on the edge," according to Canadian race walker and Olympian Iñaki Gómez, and yes he used the phrases "push the envelope" and "be on the edge" while discussing race walking.

Furthermore, the knee of the athlete's advanced leg must not bend, and the leg must straighten as the body passes over it. Each race walker is judged carefully and can be penalized if he bends his knee during the race.

Good Lord, talk about ticky-tack penalties…

Olympic distances are 20 or 50 kilometers, and both are held as road events. For some reason the 50-kilometer one is for men only, probably because the race walking dudes know they'll get beaten by the girls if they let them play. Or maybe there're all misogynists, we don't know, but there obviously must be something wrong with them.

But hold on now for a second — when was the last time you walked 50 kilometers or even used the metric system? How far is 50 kilometers anyway? So who's the nerd now? Not the race walkers. In fact, we're kind of scared of them.

Or there's another sport that's good for International Public Service Announcements for proper moisturizing and other skin care tips, including the daily use of hand lotions, creams, and salves: It's called handball, and the reason it's not important at all is because the United States has never medaled in the event. Denmark, they've medaled, and France too. Each have a bunch of gold medals. Whatever.

Handball features teams of seven players passing and dribbling a ball the size of a cantaloupe up a court that's similar to an indoor soccer field with the aim of throwing it into the opposition's goal, which happens often; spectators might see 60 goals or more in a single match.

The International Handball Federation (IHF, founded in 1946, headquartered in Basel, which is an actual town in Switzerland that makes really nice pesto) realizes this description makes their meaningful work sound totally lame so insists, through the threat of invasion of our offices by their standing robot army, that we explain how it works:

- After receiving the ball, players can only hold the ball for three seconds before passing, dribbling (like a basketball dribble), or shooting.
- After receiving the ball, players can take up to three steps…

Oh, the hell with it. No one cares, IHF! Send your busty blonde automatons to do their worst; you can't intimidate the editorial board here at our esteemed publication. You can, however, bribe us with cash.

Sorry about that. There's another unheralded Olympic event where the participating athletes simply get absolutely no action during the steamy, wee hours of the night at the Olympic Village because it seems so dorky: Trampoline.

Appearing first in the 2000 Olympics in Sydney thanks to immense pressure by the International Association of Trampoline Parks (IATP), this event features routines lasting less than a minute, and if you're a dude athlete talking to a chick athlete at an exclusive Olympic Village bar, that's just a tough sell on many levels.

Granted, competitors bounce up to 26 feet into the air, doing flips, somersaults, and twists — although it would be hilarious if they only bounced around doing somersaults or even better nothing. Just "boing, boing, boing" like a kid oh my God that would be hilarious and the commentators would just be silent or going "uhhhhhhhh" because how can you possibly backfill that with appropriate, unrealistically enthusiastic commercial-friendly commentary?

Oh, some guy from Belarus or China won the Gold Medal in Trampoline during the last Olympics. We have no idea if girls do it, and now we're tired.

The moral of the story is to watch the Summer Games because they only happen once in a while, there's a bunch of weirdly unique sports packed in there that no one pays attention to, which means they're probably actually interesting, and these athletes likely believe in their countries

more than an average citizen, given that they've
devoted their lives to representing them. Or
maybe not. It doesn't matter, they're there,
putting everything on the line and trying their
best in the face of massive judgment and critique
from people who don't know better. Especially
those folks on the trampoline. So we should take
a cue from that and do something awesome. Just
saying.

Enjoy the Games.

LOOK GOOD WHILE
SUPPORTING THE LOCAL GYM

SUMMER 2021

It's normal to want to look cool. Cool communicates a confident handle on life — an ability to adapt to any situation, overcome massive obstacles, make tons of cash, dress well, and, most importantly, act unfazed in the face of massive adversity despite wanting to just totally freak out and vomit.

This is best exemplified by the newfound universal human tendency to, with an air of almost vapid nonchalance, look busy on an iPhone while waiting in line for the restroom at a restaurant or bar, which effectively stifles the incredible, urgent, burning, panicked need to pee. Which is what cool is all about: stifling panic, and looking cool while doing so.

Thus, cool is really all about charlatanism, smoke and mirrors, and a little bit of distraction from the truth. That's why, in addition to the pee thing, humans perform all sorts of weird antics to look cool, including middle-aged people donning flat-billed baseball caps, bar owners wearing sunglasses inside, and anyone remotely associated with the technology industry driving those jelly-bean-shaped Tesla electrocars.

(Speaking of which, have you seen the size of the screen in one of those things? It looks like someone left their laptop on the dashboard. While we all wish life was more like *The Fifth Element* — or really anything with Milla Jovovich — designing cars that look like spaceships in an effort to make science fiction a reality just isn't going to work, mostly because some people actually have good taste…and maybe secretly want a Tesla real bad but are currently stuck with a faded red 2006 Subaru Forester.)

But with this cool chicanery comes vast amounts of entertainment, and there's no better place to be entertained than your local (preferably independently owned because the corporate ones are really just so lame and meathead-y, what with all the "Hey brah, get ripped, this and that" business) gym.

All sorts of people go to the gym, and it's fun to stare at them:

- 22- to 32-year-old people looking for someone to ask out
- 40-year-olds trying to reignite some ancient athletic ability

- Any person trying to lose weight
- Really athletic people
- Really obsessive people
- Senior citizens
- Personal trainers hoping their lengthy certification processes pay off
- That's it

Within this inherent diversity lies the commonality of trying to look cool while sweating and possibly grunting — excluding the senior citizens; nobody knows what they're doing there. This is because people at the gym think everyone else at the gym is always looking at them. Which they are, of course, especially if the subject is really attractive. Really attractive people are screwed, given the attention they garner. It's exhausting.

According to several recent studies, the other commonality within gym populations is the incredible lengths taken to hide what most certainly are universal bodily functions because they are decidedly uncool in public, the top three being

- perspiring
- flatulence
- belching

Gross, right? The top three subsequent remedies being

- constant toweling-off
- severe glute clenching or finding an empty

corner to stand in and look busy doing
something (there was a tie)
- forcing the burp out the nose despite the
painful head rush

Regardless of the socially required inhibition of
internal systems, folks still go to the gym
because if they don't work out they won't look
good, which is not cool. They will also die. Die
from stress. Die from Pop-Tarts. Die from loneli-
ness. Somehow they'll die. If not now, at least
in several decades. It's inevitable. But in the
short term this all explains why they suffer
through the pain of kettlebell workouts, bench
pressing, treadmills, weird stretching rituals
involving elastic bands, pull-ups, and the plank
(that isometric core exercise where one maintains
a similar position to a push-up for the maximum
possible time).

Also, secretly, the most popular activity at a
gym (according to exit polling), right after
openly ogling attractive people, is getting a
drink of water from the water fountain. This is
due to the fact that when someone is drinking
water at the water fountain, they can stop
working out for a few seconds and not be
miserable.

Other favorite gym activities include the
following:

- Searching for the right song on iTunes that
will inspire that extra rep, help you lift

that heavier weight, or drown out screams coming from the cardio equipment
- Leaving the gym to go home and lie down
- Looking in the mirror, particularly men wearing those strange, almost sideless shirts that look like the armholes got stretched out by Shaquille O'Neal
- Trying to start a conversation with the staff, who seem generally antisocial to people not also wearing a black, logoed polo shirt and trying to restock the towels

The best gyms still have wheatgrass bars from the '80s, where eventually a staff member shows up and blends the green blades into a teeny shot and people drink it and wonder why they just did that. The best gyms also have saunas that make users wonder whether or not people have sex in them, and consequently sit on a towel.

But we're off track here. The point is, looking cool actually, ironically results in ridiculous behavior that's incredibly fun to watch. And gyms are cool because they keep people in shape and not sitting at their desks or on their couches wondering why they look and feel terrible. So even though it's a hot mess in there, supporting local gyms and the human body's overall health is a good idea. Just try to avoid wearing those giant-armhole shirts — they're just not cool.

WHEN WAS THE LAST TIME YOU HIT THE TRACK?

SUMMER 2021

Horse racing takes place once a year in Kentucky and lasts about 90 seconds, at least as far as most Americans outside of Kentucky are concerned. But horse racing is a legitimate sport for people so addicted to it that they can't stop riding horses or, more commonly, frequent the facilities where the competitions transpire and get all excited about the outcome for some reason.

In fact, one of the best tennis coaches of all time — at least within the Tacoma city limits and more specifically within the property lines of the world-renowned Tacoma Lawn Tennis Club — turned out to be so committed to horse racing that (rumor had it) he hit the track every Tuesday. And, as it turns out, also on the 49 other days between May 19th and September 23rd that encompassed the live racing season at Emerald

Downs, the local gambling empire — that is, horse racing track.

This real-but-not-to-be-named great coach played tennis with a wisdom and vigor that belied his age, which may have been 37 or so at the time. Which is obviously kind of old for a top-performing athlete to still top-perform, although — thanks to extreme advances in plastic surgery, the invention of hypobaric chambers, and the increasing popularity of inversion therapy, where one hangs upside down from one's feet with the help of a contraption built specifically to hang humans upside down from their feet, which is interesting for therapeutic purposes considering it used to be a way to torture people during the Inquisition, most likely — no longer uncommon, as evidenced by the rampant success of Rafael Nadal, who is now 68 years old, and that other good-looking guy, ol' what's-his-name…oh, Roger Federer, also 68.

And Novak Djokovic, though no one really wants to talk about him because he looks like a supervillain.

But this story takes place roughly 30 years ago, when the most popular anti-aging treatments still involved SunIn® for regular people, hot oil hair treatments for rich people, and most notably, the first use of Botox, or botulinum toxin, also for rich people. That's how progress is measured: rich people turning one of the most poisonous biological substances known to humankind into a beauty product.

Botox paralyzes muscles but somehow gets rid of wrinkles, which fact actually led to the official 1997 Worldwide Shortage of Botox, where women in L.A. County took to armed but very well-dressed robbery of liquor stores for untraceable cash with which to buy slightly less effective knock-off bacteria from unscrupulous dealers, specifically Lactobacillus delbrueckii subspecies bulgaricus, which is one of the main bacteria used in the production of delicious yogurt, and thus resulted in furthering the pent-up, competitive, insecure rage of these women as their faces simply melted into deep crevasses of wrinkles as the yogurt possessed absolutely no ability to make their faces into immovable, shiny masks.

Yet yogurt usage, ironically, made them more appealing to their target audience of wealthy investment bankers since they no longer looked like expressionless Kmart mannequins. And, even more ironically, birthed the modern yogurt face cream industry, given that the inherent lactic acid dissolves dead skin cells and what's more serves as an all-around beauty multitasker as it (the yogurt) moisturizes, fights acne, prevents premature aging (a term which actually has no definition), relieves sunburn, and reduces discoloration. According to the yogurt beauty product manufacturing industry at least.

Nonetheless, our storied '90s-era coach of approximately 37 years coached pretty well, used to play up to the satellite tennis tournament level pretty well, and loved trifectas.

In professional tennis, satellite circuits were four-week tournaments for players outside the top few hundred ATP rankings where they, if successful, could move on to top-flight ATP Tour events. It's the tennis tournament version of "so you're saying there's a chance" for folks looking to go pro. Nowadays it's known as the ITF World Tennis Tour, representing the lowest rung of the professional tennis ladder. Nearly every professional player has spent time on the ITF World Tennis Tour.

Which brings up another story about another highly localized best tennis coach of all time, who was a great athlete and used to walk into the Tacoma Lawn Tennis Club—hosted PNW Open — the largest tennis tournament in the Pacific Northwest, with $50,000 in prize money at stake (singles champions earn somewhere in the neighborhood of four grand), and a tournament that in 2017 chose to close the gender wage gap by awarding equal prize money to both men and women though it's just insane to think it took that long and reflect upon all the years where the women got paid less based on the fact that they are women — with his shirt off. That's just awesome.

Anyway, this shirtless, ripped coach borrowed a bunch of money from club members to go hit the satellite circuit, where he didn't find success, and ended up not paying any of it back and getting a job installing those steel mesh cages/bulletproof partitions in cop cars that separate the back seat from the front. To prevent attacks and shootings and stabbings and such.

Which just goes to show how hard it is to go pro as a great tennis player, or a cop.

It turns out horse racing is a hot-button issue for many folks, particularly at PETA, but it's currently still a sport, as evidenced by the following realities:

- Jockeys endure regular fitness regimens like any pro athlete, with the added pressure of maintaining full control of their diet as horses are allocated a specific weight to carry in a race. Jockeys weigh on average between 108 and 118 pounds and lead 1200-pound horses upwards of 40 miles per hour, so it's not just about being lightweight, it's about balancing weight with strength like a gymnast. Dang!

Update: A gymnast we know stated, "They are holding a contraction in their quads, hamstrings, and glutes for the duration of the race, while the horse is going forty miles per hour. Not even a gymnast can do that."

- Horses' enormous aerobic capacity allowed various ancient warriors like the one we did a report on in high school, Alexander the Great (and his horse, Bucephalus), to range thousands of miles and subjugate those populations lacking horses or contemporary weapons technology — or leaders with cool names. The point is, despite their innate desire to avoid danger, horses' intense competitive spirit melds with skilled, horse whispering—type training to create a pretty awesome, albeit nonhuman, athlete.

- A session bringing the horse to a fast gallop to test its speed and fitness is called a "work" or "breeze." The workouts can be timed by a clocker and can be published in industry papers and track programs. This allows potential buyers and people placing wagers to see how the horse has been performing up to a given race. Which brings up some interesting points…

1. Much like what happened with the 2017 FBI investigation into college basketball corruption (missed that? don't worry, everyone did) or on a more lighthearted (sort of) note the whole Deflategate thing, federal investigators have used surveillance to catch people putting perform-ance-enhancing drugs (PEDs) in horses. For exam-ple, in 2020 the trainer of the world's best thoroughbred racehorse was indicted on federal charges for participating in a doping scheme.

2. As in all the sports we love (think Major League Baseball, currently enforcing rules around pitchers' cheating by using "sticky balls"), there are some unsavory characters involved in horse racing, including corrupt "coaches" and ownership, low-level hustlers, and gambling enterprises attempting to influence the outcomes. But it's really no different than in any other sporting situation.

Ultimately horse racing is a social activity that draws in people who enjoy the communal aspect of watching races. It's essentially a day-long social event punctuated by exciting races. Plus there's the whole fashion thing, what with the gigantic hats and other ridiculousness, a.k.a. the horse racing equivalent of face painting for a football or basketball game, or waving those continent-sized flags at a soccer match.

If managed and led correctly, horse racing can be a great educator and encourage a sense of responsibility toward caring for animals and respecting the beauty and agility of the racehorse as an athlete. Making us better humans overall, in theory.

So hit the track. Do some (legal) wagering. Have a beer. Check out something you haven't seen before. Life is short and complicated, but the horses don't care and the race is fairly simple, and we could all use more simplicity.

WRESTLE WITH WHAT KIND OF COMPETITOR YOU ARE

SUMMER 2021

The mentality of competition, otherwise known as competitiveness, or in some cases sports psychology, allowed me to win the Seattle Half Marathon in 2002. Or maybe it was 2003. And technically it's called The Amica Insurance Seattle Half Marathon, and technically I didn't win it. I merely finished. Which was a win for me.

If how we compete in our brain pans weren't important, Coach Pete Carroll and Dr. Michael Gervais wouldn't have founded their online and corporate educational platform Compete to Create to "develop the team skills and mindset to succeed and innovate." This platform is for other people, not them; Pete and Mike pretty much have competing down.

I'm not sure this makes sense — "succeed and innovate" sounds kind of vague. How about "kill and destroy"? That's a bit more specific.

Anyway, I'm sure it's legit. It's "mindset training used by the world's top high performing leaders, from Olympians to Fortune 100 executives, to A-list celebrities and…" Damn, wait a second, A-list celebrities too? I'm in! I don't want to be hanging around with no mentally messed-up, low-performing B-list celebrity, no way. I side with the winning team, thank you very much. I'm going over to Compete to Create right now with my highlight reel and list of accolades — none of which are verifiable — to sign up. Or maybe ask for a job teaching; I'm obviously super good at it.

If you examine their offerings, there's some cool stuff in there, like the foundational course "Finding Your Best," which results ("upon successful completion" — meaning people who don't finish the course successfully are instantly electroshocked through their keyboards — it's a virtual course now — which is actually way better than the previous punishment, er, re-education strategy of verbal taunts and shaming by the good doctor and Pete themselves, in a rubber room, with uncomfortable chairs) in the receipt of a nifty and exclusive (unless you know a good graphic designer) "Compete to Create High Performance Mindset Badge to showcase on LinkedIn or share on social networks."

Speaking of which, there's all sorts of crazy words in here — "here" being their website — words I don't understand but seem important, including "mindfulness," "high-performance mindset training," "ignite," "activate your potential," "accelerate"… Whoa now, just hold on a second, accelerate? That sounds dangerous. Maybe this isn't for me, even though, in all seriousness, I bet the course is very helpful, and for $499.00 I'd pay for a look inside Carroll's and Gervais's brains.

Back to the point: Competitiveness is an affliction of the human brain that allows folks to supersede any preternatural ability, manage pain, and accomplish things they, when not in a competitive state, may consider unaccomplishable.

This obviously applies to sports. Which really wasn't obvious until my 1997 smash hit college thesis, "Victory in Sports Is Often Attributed to Wanting to Win," garnered so many awards — the most prominent of which was my diploma in English Literature, something literally no one has ever asked to see and/or verify (thank goodness, because I'm not sure I ever received an actual copy) — that the issue of competitiveness was thrown into the media spotlight, including a special airing of *30 for 30* on ESPN that is entirely fictional but I wish happened.

And it's weird to think that if I'd had half a brain, I could have just hung out during those college years instead of paying tuition and going to class. Maybe doing some sweaty, shirtless carpentry work in the summers for really attractive, wealthy women — kind of like that pool guy situation from the music video "Tease Me, Please Me" by Scorpions — but nothing weird would happen with the lady I swear and anyway I'd just make some cash money while still learning stuff, maybe absorbing lessons from friends actually going to college. Then I'd "graduate" and go get that crappy job at a PR firm, despite not having actually gone to college and it doesn't matter anyway because my boss isn't ever going to ask to look at my diploma and geez see how much money I saved by not paying tuition?

Competitiveness is a big deal. The brain part of it is, at least. There's two main kinds of competitiveness, and one is good and one is bad so if you have the bad one you should really look into self-improvement courses, several of which I can sell you. Don't worry about it right now stay focused but email me later if you're interested the whole thing is done with Dogecoin.

The first kind of competitiveness is a gearshift. It's a drivetrain in the human brain and soul that inspires action. This action is associated with one focused goal, and any impediments to achieving this goal are recognized yet (here's the trick) not focused upon, as on an average day when idiotic, annoying obstacles arise and we're all bent out of shape and exasperated and geek-stressed, like

"#%*$amn it, why is the coffee maker broken again?" or

"They said the wait for a table is forty-five minutes" or

"My Apple Watch wonnnnnt't updattttttte, mwahhhhh."

The latter of which may or may not accurately reflect the mindset of the author a few days ago.

Nay, with the good kind of competitive mindset, or gear, impediments and obstacles are quickly identified but not perseverated upon, thanks to this weird juice that flows throughout our neurosystems in this competitive state where our singular focus transforms us into obstacle-overcoming machines.

That's it. That's our purpose in that moment. Overcome the obstacle. Which could be a broken backboard on a hoop or playing one-on-one against someone six inches taller than us. It could be working on lactic thresholds over months to increase our endurance for a triathlon or hitting a heavy bag so many times we want to throw up but our trainer is asking for more. No ego, no self-pity, just focus: win.*

*Sometimes we try to shift to this mindset at a bar while shooting into one of those miniature basketball hoops or playing foosball, but it doesn't work because of the beer. Or spicy margaritas. Or whatever.

We all have this good kind of competitiveness. For special folks like Simone Biles, it leads to a higher mental state that provides a tremendous capacity for both fitness and this unfathomable amount of focus that facilitates the insane (and life-threatening) stuff gymnasts are wont to do. But for the rest of us, it just gets us off our rears to do something without complaining.

The second kind of competitiveness is awful and couldn't be more opposite from the good-person kind. This second one is all about ego and status and superiority complexes. There's no gearshift with this version; it's a trait, which is why it rears its ugly head in the form of unsolicited and unwanted discussions of salary, vacations, apps (yes, as in a "so cool" iPhone app), various past triumphs (sporting or otherwise, ugh this one is just so lame), great meals, subtle and unsubtle put-downs about something someone else accomplished, vehicles, politics, and (most notably) the perpetrator listening to a story from whoever is in the room then promptly recounting a similar story, albeit an ostensibly better version.

Granted, there are actual accomplishments in there that likely came about through a healthy dose of the first kind of competitiveness — which is laudable. Unfortunately, the second kind of competitiveness holds sway, and consequently the accomplishment part falls on deaf ears.

So this is a call to identify what kind of competitive mindset you have. Is it the one that allows you to focus and do cool stuff, even if you're defeated? Or is it the one that involves stepping on other people's toes all the time, which you explain away by just thinking you're obligated, by your very nature, to compete, and most importantly win, always?

The truth of the matter is, once we peel it all back, it may take a while but everybody loves a loser because we can see ourselves in them. Winners, on the other hand...well, winners who always have to win are hard to like. It's helpful to throw a good dose of empathy at them, though.

See you in class.

THE HEALTH, WELLNESS, AND FITNESS INDUSTRIES FACE A HUGE MARKETING PROBLEM

SUMMER 2021

The thing the makers of Peloton, who we think are called "Peloton," don't disclose on a big sticker like they should is that if we ride that stupid bike for months on end and still drink delicious, hazy IPAs from Oregon, Washington, or (if really lucky) Vermont every night, we still end up with the physique of a fat slob. Unless we're one of those lucky people with the completely illogical discipline to eat small portions and not love beer, in order to stay healthy, as recommended by the World Health Organization (WHO), American Medical Association (AMA), and, more dastardly, the National Fitness Professionals Association (NFPA), complete with their suggestive tan lines, unattainably sculpted abdomens, and overall propensity for energy and happiness.

Or one of those folks with naturally fast metabolisms and otherwise low-body-fat biological metrics, whom we consistently try not to become enraged at.

This same gross communicative disservice applies to the manufacturers (or, more specifically, their non-moral-compass-having marketing departments) of NordicTrack Treadmills, Stairmaster Stepmill Torture Devices, Bowflex Home Gyms (with all the weird pulleys), Lululemon Mirror Home Gyms (giant iPhone-looking things that reflect a trainer, poltergeists, and a fatter version of ourselves back at us), Planet Fitness buildings, and various CrossFit locations.

The other thing these folks might want to mention or at least forewarn us about is the incredibly difficult transition from the equipment they make or house to the real world. Meaning, going for a run on the concrete — what with the wind and the dogs and the hills and the traffic and the heat and the sweat and the neighbors pointing and laughing — is much more difficult than running on a treadmill, alone, in the basement, at a respectable 12-minute mile while listening to Mötley Crüe's "Kickstart My Heart" and taking frequent water breaks.

Although, upon further review, along with the potential for getting to look at attractive instructors, interacting with fitness equipment, apps, or franchises increases self-esteem and results in better moods, thanks to a combination of endorphins — hormones and neuro-signaling molecules that function as painkillers, which riding an exercise bike while staring at a hot person boosts production of — and being around other humans, i.e., a sense of community. Huh.

Yet there's still a communication breakdown to discuss, one that is not unlike the marketing malfeasance inherent in the stand-up paddleboard (SUP) manufacturing industry. The most popular SUP brands completely, intentionally misrepresent the inherent difficulty and overall impossibleness of standing up on the wildly unstable flotsam, as evidenced by their various stability-suggestive monikers, including Stand on Liquid, Pathfinder, Goplus, Boardworks Surf, Don't Worry You'll Never Fall and Die, and the laid-back, hang-loose, chill-out, island-styled Pau Hana.

In fact, the only paddleboard brand communicating in our true best interest here is iROCKER.

Stand-up paddleboarding is impossible. We spent six long miles on a river in Oregon, lying on our stomach, eyes closed, desperately clinging to some off-brand, rented SUP, while the tumultuous current of the upper Deschutes River raged around us and young families with small children slowly bobbed on by in inner tubes, rafts, and floaties, giving us the strangest open-mouthed stares/bemused expressions, given the inherent danger of the situation. The only reason our wife and kid got up on their boards was due to their incredible, almost Olympic-caliber athletic abilities — which, when it comes to the kid, we hope to profit from some day.

Although, upon further review, paddleboarding increases core strength, which consequently increases overall stability and posture, thereby lessening common afflictions like back and neck pain. Huh again. Plus there's the whole "mental clarity because there's no screen in your face" part.

Nonetheless, there are more health and wellness branding flaws to discuss, and none are more flawed than the conglomerates behind the mass-production of Yoga Instructors — virtual or otherwise — who also routinely communicate with malintent and bait-and-switch-like maneuvers. The thousands of prime-time commercials we see (we don't have cable, and streaming Netflix and Hulu is far too overwhelming) feature supple, lithe instructors of various sexes with perfectly calm countenances bending and reaching and downward-dogging without a bead of sweat in sight while not only still breathing but actually carrying on a conversation that essentially revolves around pushing out the jive and bringing in the love.

We can attest that the semisexual act of performing yoga itself makes this effortless posturing extraordinarily difficult to mirror, which is why the ads are always shot from the back of the class, thus hiding the grimacing, strained, terror-ridden expressions of the non-bendy, civilian participants (although, just like in school, there's always a few overachievers who perform various poses with relative ease, largely inspired by their propensity for sycophancy). Indeed, real yoga involves extreme amounts of sweat, tremulous appendages, and constant concern about the potential emanation of various bodily noises, including crying.

Although, upon further review, studies show people who take up yoga-ing lose five pounds, decrease blood pressure, lower bad cholesterol, and in general find space for self-awareness, kindness, self-compassion, and a bunch of other things that seem made up. More power to them.

Wait. Rock climbing, specifically the Indoor Rock Climbing Consortium, also propagates misinformation regarding the relative ease of use and ignores the fact that climbing things involves altitudes deemed generally unsafe for humans, since we don't all have jetpacks yet. Our fit, thin, overly strong young neighbors down the street are obviously brainwashed by the nefarious producers and promoters of climbing, given that they recently discussed our local chapter of this syndicate and even suggested we give it a try as "anyone can do it and they show you how."

Just imagine the unsightly chalked hands, finger pain, and toe cramps likely involved — none of which are highlighted by our neighborhood "Premier Rock-Climbing Destination," which instead advertises "Intro Classes," "Gift Cards," and "Youth Summer Camps." The gall of it all takes our breath away.

Although, upon further review, climbing apparently involves low-impact movements that don't focus on repetition or only the sagittal plane — which the National Academy of Sports Medicine

(NASM) defines as forward and backward movements based on dividing the body into left and right parts — but also include the frontal plane (side-to-side movements) and the transverse plane (twisting movements), which is the best way to train. Not to mention honing problem-solving skills and increasing confidence from literally overcoming a hard, rocky obstacle. Huh. Who knew?

Let this be a lesson in awareness. It turns out the marketing for workouts, training, or general fitness pastimes that involve moving our bodies can be wildly inaccurate to the point of negligence. Yet turn off that noise, give new stuff a try, and see what works — you may be surprised by the result.

SHAMELESS PROMOTION OF PENDLETON, OREGON

SUMMER 2021

Pendleton, Oregon, is a town that's far away from
Seattle and fairly far away from Portland and
really far away from Portland, Maine, a town that
no one has ever been to but is apparently
surrounded by 40,000 acres of wild blueberries.
Surrounded in the sense that the state of Maine
itself propagates this vast quantity of blueberry
foliage, which turns out to be the favorite food
of black bears, foxes, deer, rabbits, skunks, fox
squirrels, chipmunks, and really liberal college
students — all of which, in combination, explains
why no one ever goes to Portland, Maine. At least
in a touristic sense.

But remember: we're talking about Pendleton,
Oregon, here, not Maine, so try to focus.
Pendleton is located in the wilds of Northeastern

Oregon, nestled in the valley of the Umatilla River and surrounded by vast tracts of golden wheat fields and little truck stop—like centers that usually have a Carl's Jr. or some other "it sounded like a good idea but now I feel gross" quasi-famous fast food chain. It has hot, dry summers and fairly short, cool winters that supposedly generate 15 inches of snow per year, but how is that actually tracked and measured? With a ruler? And who's recording this? Are they trained in anything beyond ruler-holding? Sounds like a scam to bring in those tourists Portland (Maine) so desperately craves.

Speaking of tourists, our sources recently visited Pendleton and confirmed the presence of the Pendleton Round-Up Grandstand, which immediately begs an explanation of why our sources were there and what, exactly, a grandstand is. Our sources were there to connect with a shipment of 1,000 pounds of Brazilian cocaine (ironically) smuggled by a Columbian cartel, which is why we shouldn't have mentioned this. And a grandstand is a structure for seating spectators of auto racing, horse racing, or rodeo events — it is, in essence, a single section of stadium but further differs from a whole stadium in that it does not wrap all or most of the way around because the people who watch auto racing and horse racing are generally claustrophobic. Fact.

The existence of the Pendleton Round-Up Grandstand adequately explains the prevalence of independent retailers located throughout town specializing in cowboy and cowgirl stuff, a.k.a. "Western wear," many of which paid us to mention their names — specifically Hamley & Co. Western Store, ReRide Western Re-sale Store, and Staplemans Custom Cowboy & Cowgirl Boots and Shoes, the latter of which is very popular amongst people with a chaps fetish because they sell tons of chaps, chaps being sturdy coverings buckled over trousers with an integrated belt but, unlike trousers, lacking a seat and not joined at the crotch. Thus the fetish. Although the original intent of these strange pants was to allow those cowboys and cowgirls to ride horses and bulls and (when no one is looking) lions from the local zoo — and otherwise protect their legs from ranch-style environmental hazards like working with livestock and sagebrush and stuff. Oh, and no one paid us to mention their names — we're hoping, however, that they somehow see this article and mail us a check. We like our chances.

The existence of the Pendleton Round-Up Grand-stand also explains the Pendleton Round-Up itself — the over 100-year-old major rodeo held every year (except, of course, in 2020 but returning this year, September 15—18, 2021) — adding upwards of 50,000 chaps enthusiasts of various persuasions to the town's 17,000 residents. It's pure madness. Main Street converts from wheeled traffic to horse-traffic-only, there's a dress-up parade that implies a certain amount of kinkiness goes on, a kick-off concert, a "Happy Canyon" show (live retelling of Pendleton's founding and other local history), the largest annual teepee village encampment honoring the history of the Umatilla Native American tribe, and (off the record) whiskey swigging, fistfights, light gunplay after being accused "a cheat" in saloon-style poker games on dirty tables with puffy dress—wearing prostitutes lounging about various banisters…and, of course, the Round-Up itself, which is where the athletics comes in.

The Pendleton Round-Up is a member of the Professional Rodeo Cowboys Association (PRCA) and pays out $337,500 in prize money to the crazy maniacs who compete in Bareback Bronc Riding, Saddle Bronc Riding, Bull Riding, Steer Roping, Steer Wrestling, Naked Oil Wrestling, Team Roping, and Tie-Down Roping as both a trade and profession. Other events include Barrel Racing, Six-Shooter Bank Robbing with Getaway, Breakaway Roping, and Wild Cow Milking. That's right, wild cow milking. The whole thing is a PETA and possibly World Wildlife Fund nightmare, but when we think about it lots of things are.

The Pendleton Round-Up's catchphrase/branding tagline "Let 'er Buck" accurately describes most of what professional cowboys and cowgirls do. But in fact, both the humans and the livestock need to be in peak condition to compete. Plus it's a team sport, given that the very nature of rodeo requires a working relationship/partnership between the cowboys/girls and the animal athletes. Any cowgirl/boy will tell you they take home a paycheck only when both they and the animal are in top form. And when the animal is slacking, the human partner is forced to have difficult yet supportive conversations about what the heck is going on — coined "bull whispering" due to the bull's natural tendency to bottle up its emotions or otherwise avoid situations where it feels vulnerable.

The factors separating the top athletes from the rest of the field are the same as in any pro sport, those being raw talent, the desire to win, mental fitness, attractiveness on a score of 1 to 10, hundreds of hours spent developing sport-specific skills, and extraordinarily high levels of fitness. To the latter point, pro rodeo-ers focus on core strength, overall strength training, lactic threshold improvement (as do endurance athletes), and anything else that develops high levels of aerobic fitness as their heartrates are extremely elevated long before and long after a ride (not just during the 8-second run on a bucking horse or bull).

There's even a state-of-the-art workout facility in Decatur, Texas, called Fit-N-Wise that Jerry Jones likely owns, with a rodeo sports performance program that caters to the best cowboys in the world and tries to sell them PEDs in back rooms. Power, agility explosiveness, and foot-speed are all emphasized with pro football—styled workouts like leg cradles, leg raises, lunges, kettlebell swings, medicine ball work, and tire flips — to name a few.

Speaking of football, there's a former NFL player who joined the PRCA as a steer wrestler with much success: former New York Giants tight end Bear (real name, talk about being destined for football and/or rodeo-ing) Pascoe (several receptions in the Super Bowl XLVI upset of the New England Patriots — yay! — not to reveal our bias, oops). Note: Bear was not involved in the helmet catch.

The 6'5", 260-pound Pascoe "finished the money" in the steer wrestling title race at the Ellensburg, Washington, Rodeo, which offers competitors $341,885 in prize money. He compares steer wrestling to pro football in some ways:

"Both are very high-tempo, very physical sports. In steer wrestling you're dealing with three animals and two humans, so a lot can happen. At least on a football field, most guys can kind of judge what a team's going to do or what a defense is going to do. There's a lot more variables when you're steer wrestling."

Good grief. Don't tell Gronk about the PRCA, please. We love that guy but it's just, you know, it would be nice to not see him win yet another title in…anything. Not to show our bias against Tampa Bay. Oops!

The message here is the following: Pendleton, Oregon, is a real place you should visit to watch cowboys, cowgirls, and their animal partners — a.k.a. top-notch athletes — perform at a high level. Plus you may get to see some bar fights where someone is picked up, smashed on top of half-full drink glasses, and slid down the length

of the bar to crash in a heap next to the musta-
chioed, striped shirt—wearing barkeep. Oh, and
Portland, Maine, is to be avoided. And we're
totally open to advertising your business within
long-form copy.

See you at the Round-Up.

PROFANITY IS THE HALLMARK
OF HIGH PERFORMANCE

SUMMER 2021

The hard part about hiring a sports icon to market various products or services is that one doesn't ever know when the sports icon is going to freak out and swear like a Hell's Angel or some other miscreant whom a corporation that's trying to appeal to mass markets certainly does not want to associate itself with.

For example, tennis star Jimmy Connors — that homespun, almost generic-seeming Captain America of professional tennis from roughly 1972 to 1996 — had some uniquely disparaging comments for former cyborg Ivan Lendl after losing a game to him at the 1992 U.S. Open, comments that we can't repeat here but many of which involved words that begin with *f*, followed by the oddly phrased "-playing pusher," which most certainly made luxury-ish clothing brand Sergio Tacchini, one of Connors's biggest sponsors, somewhat nervous, although back then maybe not, who knows? It was a long time ago.

We expected nothing less from former tennis great and now-ubiquitous major tournament announcer John McEnroe, given his penchant for throwing explosive tantrums on the court every five minutes, combined with the fact that he just looks pissed off all the time, including while delivering commentary at Wimbledon. Although you may be surprised to discover that in 1983 McEnroe called his opponent Tomás Smid a "communist bastard" at a Forest Hills event. Smid, a Czechoslovakian, and his fans were furious at the remark despite the accuracy of the "communist" part, given that Czechoslovakia was a satellite state of the Soviet Union back then. Although the Cold War was no excuse for causing innocents, like ourselves, to blush.

In the early 2000s, a great seat at a (relatively) small tournament revealed to our sources that Andre Agassi's favorite self-flagellation technique for poor performance was emitting a litany of vile, profane, and psychologically unhelpful comments while slapping his left thigh. And obviously this shocking behavior is not confined to tennis — anyone who's seen Michael Jordan in *The Last Dance* on ESPN knows that the world's former foremost product endorser cussed like a sailor on the court/in the locker room/driving his Ferrari/buying yogurt/during a

Hanes underwear ad shoot. In fact, airing *The Last Dance* was the first and only time The Walt Disney Company (part owner of ESPN) even vaguely associated itself with such odious language outside of the Disney employee break room behind Space Mountain, likely because Jordan actually bought the Federal Communications Commission (FCC) in 1999 and ESPN in 2002 thanks to his various Wheaties/Hanes/McDonald's/Coca-Cola promotional contracts, so they had to do it his way.

Indeed, these same traits exist in all present-day highly marketable sports icons,* from (sigh) Tom Brady to Kyle Busch (the NASCAR guy, come on, watch some other sports once in a while, sheesh) to Katie Ledecky to Cristiano Ronaldo, and don't forget Nelly Korda (come on, six-time champion on the LPGA Tour) — these traits being broad appeal with consumers and mouths like drunk, NoDoz-addled truckers.

*The one exception is Russell Wilson — we'd all love to hear him drop some horrific language occasionally, just so we know his apparent niceness is balanced out with a realistic amount of normalness or at least not-boringness. He's obviously not boring on the field, it's just that Seahawks fans are secretly nervous that he's a dud off the field, like not fun to hang out with, because it seems like this just might be the case.

It turns out swearing and sports and/or swearing as a part of competition is a natural phenomenon wired into the human brain for several purely biological/instinctual reasons. The first reason is that guys need to look cool in front of babes. From an early age (like about the sixth grade), anyone into babes realizes that using profanity makes one appear more mature and cooler overall, which, generally speaking, is something babes like. This is also why there are so many after-school specials with a babe who's into the "bad" person — those attractive folks whose swearing and smoking and preference for leather jackets makes them even more attractive in the eyes of babes — and these "bad" people are, of course, in the "greasers" or some other gang that doesn't actually do criminally bad things, just bad things as defined by the mores of the '50s, specifically swearing, smoking, and donning leather jackets. Oh, maybe some drinking too.

But eventually the babe realizes the error of her ways since it turns out "bad" behavior is a one-way ticket to Loserville, and the afterschool special concludes with the babe going out with the milquetoast, quiet, do-gooding nerd. Which is frustrating as this never happens in real life. But the point is, one of the reasons afterschool specials exist is to try and get junior high kids off profanity, which they use to impress people they like. Also, all afterschool specials are produced by Pat Robertson's Christian Broad-casting Network (CBN), so that might be part of it too.

The second reason is that swearing increases pain tolerance. Which is why so many married couples have potty mouths. Researchers from the U.K.'s Keele University — which is an actual place rather than a set design from Harry Potter — had "participants" stick their hands in ice-cold water and cuss, then do it again using non-offensive words. The research team found that "swearing increased pain tolerance, increased heart rate, and decreased perceived pain compared with not swearing" and that "sticking someone's hand in ice-cold water makes them want to punch you in the mouth, which they do if you're not paying attention."

Also, it turns out these "researchers" were actually rogue employees from the University's maintenance department, but the study proved so exciting and valid-seeming in the sports psychology world that good ol' Keele U covered it up by granting the janitors full tenure (with some help from Prince Harry and Meghan Markle).

How, exactly, swearing increases pain tolerance these researchers did not cover since they suddenly had to start publishing research papers. But they chalked a theory suggesting the use of bad words is linked to humans' fight-or-flight response. In this sexy mode, hormones are released to help the body react to possible danger. This state can help people perform in tough situations, including those involving physical pain or discomfort. Furthermore, the accelerated heart rates of the "volunteers" who swore indicates increased aggression, which is something all animals show to "downplay feebleness" or, in more scientific terms, "not look like lunch," i.e., to appear stronger and more pain-tolerant to deter threats, which could be in the form of a larger rhinoceros if you're a rhinoceros but more likely, in our cases, is a buffer dude talking to our woman, or whomever we orient to or whatnot.

The third reason is that swear words land directly in our brains as a distraction method to take our minds off how awful something is (cue married couple setting household budgets or any audience member witnessing the Broadway produc-tion of *Beetlejuice*). Some guy employed by Long Island University — we're not sure in what capacity — co-authored a swearing and exercise study and found that "there's a disinhibition in play that causes individuals to perform better while swearing." Which no one understood, so he translated it to "Put simply, when swearing we are no longer focused on the discomfort caused by the activity or exercise we are engaged in."

Aha! That's it! Profanity is the equivalent of taking a Jäger shot after your partner dumps you because you still drink Jäger shots and don't have a job. Which may have happened to us but, like the Cold War, that was a long time ago.

So if you're seeking higher performance, maybe you're negotiating your bonus, playing a pickup half-court game at the park, attending a parent-teacher conference, or negotiating a lease on one of those Mercedes Sprinters, it's likely time to start dropping as much truly offensive, profan-ity-laden language as possible to crush your opponents and get what you want. If anyone complains, just refer them to this article. The science is there: Swearing is just a part of who you are. A winner.

YOU'RE NOT LIVING IF YOU'RE NOT BLASTING AWAY AT DOVES

SUMMER 2021

Mourning doves are murderous, evil little birds bent on our destruction. They fly onto our windowsills at night like stalkers, attempting to peek between our blinds with their beady little black eyes to determine our specific location, report it back to the flock, then find a weak spot in our domiciles (typically plumbing vents, chimneys, windows teenagers leave open despite repeated conversations about the importance of closing them "because we said so," and doggie doors) and attack in a "swarm o' doves," as the phrase goes, ineffectually pecking at us with their teeny-tiny beaks, yet truly bringing terror to our souls.

Which is exactly why Washington State, and likely many other, slightly less cool states, established an annual mourning dove hunting season

where apparently mostly men (okay, only men,
which is lame as the last thing any party needs
is the arrival of yet another car full of dudes)
show up in camouflage despite the fact that
mourning doves are not overly bright and will fly
within feet of the human head, then promptly land
12 yards away and start pecking for seeds in an
almost absent-minded fashion. Meaning the camouflage is entirely unnecessary. You could hunt
mourning doves in a Mariner Moose costume or a
construction worker's neon orange safety gear.
Speaking of which, moose as a species are a relatively recent arrival to Washington. They started
showing up from Canada or Idaho or some other
place where the Wildlings live around 1977,
presumably with bad cases of Disco Fever and thus
looking for a place to spend their Boogie Nights.
Now there are conflicting reports of the local
moose population (mostly in Northeastern Washington State, or any part of the state where gun
ownership starts at roughly age 14). Some parts
of the Internet say their numbers total 5,000,
others 400, but either way pay heed — there's
nothing worse than trying to figure out how to
get a foraging, lackadaisical, slightly sleepy
moose, Snoop Dogg, or Sam Perkins out of your
yard/car/garage.

The dove season typically opens September 1st every
year — a truly great day for mankind, just saying
— making it the first time people get to blast
away at living things since about January. Hopefully. Although there are some spring seasons for
things like turkey (total opposite of doves, one

has to be completely camouflaged, including the face, and completely motionless in a blind to harvest a turkey; also, there is no greater contrast than choking down some wild turkey as compared to the coddled, overfed, slightly anxious, couch-bound, farm-raised Butterball variety we're all used to — we also have it on good authority that Italians think turkey is "a dirty bird" and thus don't eat it, which may be the best thing ever), cougar (stop it, we mean the predatory giant cat), rabbit, bobcat, and fox. We like to think farmers or people with land actually hunt cougar, rabbit, bobcat, and fox; that makes it seem more normal, as opposed to, well, some guy who lives by himself in an apartment downtown. Yikes.

The best part about dove hunting is the weather. Our recent visit to Moses Lake in Eastern Washington featured shorts, T-shirts, and multiple showers from the heat, which is much better than walking around like the Michelin Man and falling down in icy parking lots. Even at dawn the temperature was 55°, pretty sweet.

The other best part about dove hunting is that, unlike other hunting experiences, it has great potential for actual shooting. Avid hunters don't care for it thanks to the aforementioned overall, ah, let's call it "lack of focus" and "general inattentiveness" inherent in the birds. Some people prefer game that pits man-wit to game-wit, requires careful stalking or luring with decoys (like duck), or could result in man-death if one isn't careful (bear, both kinds of cougars).

Others, like us, enjoy the opportunity for shooting, and mourning doves supply shooting opportunities in droves.

These birds do have one thing going for them: they fly in such irregular patterns it's like trying to hit a honeybee with a quarter. They're actually founding members of the International Aerobatic Club (IAC) — they bob and weave, rotate longitudinally (roll) and laterally (pitch), accelerate and decelerate rapidly, wear little red scarves, goggles, and old-timey leather flight caps, and, like any good stunt pilot, know when to leave a smoke trail — which, upon investigation, comes from the aircraft pumping biodegradable, paraffin-based oil directly onto hot exhaust nozzles (piston engines), exhaust fumes (jet engines), or, in the case of doves, a simple ignition of their butt fumes.

This airborne agility must be why some dove hunters insist on shooting gigantic semi-automatic 12-gauge shotguns with three-inch shells despite the fact that a dove weighs about five ounces and spans 12 inches in length, roughly three to four of which are the tail. For non-gun-wielding-enthusiasts, the "gauge" of a shotgun refers to the diameter of the barrel/size of the shell. Twelve is big, 10 is biggest (inversely proportionate), 20 is an all-arounder, and 28 is getting small (but perfect for doves).

The other reason may be that new shotguns are expensive, and given that dove season technically runs for two months but peters out within three weeks because as soon as the temperature drops to about 50° overnight doves hightail it to Mexico because they're essentially beach bums and love margaritas — leaving us the three-month-long, frigid duck and goose season where we sit in blinds shivering and telling ourselves this is, overall, a good idea and worth missing birthdays and Seahawks games over and that shooting a duck with anything less than a 12-gauge (okay, 20-gauges work) is not a good recipe for duck pie (yum) — one can't afford, financially or practically, to buy a new, smaller gun just for dove. More's the pity.

Oh! A third best part about dove hunting is ease of use. Due to doves' evolutionary idiocy, there are two primary methods. The first is to stand under some nice-looking willow, or any available tree fit for bird sleeping, at dusk. As they fly in to roost, you shoot. And miss and curse and try not to think about how much it just cost to pull the trigger, given that the price of a box of shells is about $25.00, or $1.00 per pull. The second is to stand (or preferably sit in a folding chair) in a crop field at dawn, ideally within a few hundred yards of those nice-looking trees, then try and track and shoot the lightning-fast silhouettes of the doves as they fly in for breakfast. Good luck. There is a third method that involves flapping your arms and stomping around a field at noon, bending over to peck at seeds while making soothing cooing sounds, but that's the kind of specialized thing only the really well-seasoned folks do.

The limit for dove is 15. During our hunt at Moses Lake we got four and missed about nine, which we were fine with. Given their tininess, one needs about 10 doves for a three-setting meal, so we donated ours to this dude who said he'd feed his family and the neighbors with them. Doves are quite delicious — we'd say dove and pheasant are the best-eating game birds. Ironically (based on the larger opportunity to get 'em), duck are the worst. We encourage smoking them or otherwise dividing them up and mixing them with other proteins to make it work — as with turkey, wild duck is a far cry from the obese, farm-raised monsters one eats in a restaurant.

Oh! The final best parts about dove hunting include these:

- Following the guy who knows where to go in a careening caravan on country roads in the dark at breakneck speeds. All hunters are paranoid they'll lose their "spot," even if it's on their own land, so everyone's always in a hurry to get there.
- Being the only one without a gigantic Ford F-150, -250, or -350 and thinking you'll get stuck in the weird, powdery, sand-like dirt that comprises unirrigated Eastern Washington soil.
- Not telling your wife how dirty her car got.
- Cleaning your gun in the hotel room when you're done, as weird as that feels.

There's something soothing about the smell of gun oil. Trust us.

For the record, we're kidding about the blasting away stuff. Hunting and shooting is an art and a skill that takes practice and most importantly deserves your respect and attention. It's challenging, and it's fun.

So now you know what to do September 1, 2022. We don't care if you have other plans or don't want to do it or think it's barbaric or whatever. You're booked. We'll see you there. You'll love it, trust us. And bring some snacks to share, okay? We get hungry out there standing in the field.

PROPRIOCEPTION AND THE MENTAL HEALTH BENEFITS OF WINTER SPORTS

FALL 2021

When people move to the Pacific Northwest from states that don't feature 226 to 308 days a year with clouds covering upwards of 75% of the sky, they frequently freak out and want to move back to Napa, which is fine by Pacific Northwesterners, not that we have anything in particular against Napians other than their teeming wealth and lack of Seasonal Affective Disorder, which they will acquire after their first Thanksgiving here.

It's best to warn Californians researching real estate through indulgent, in-real-life tours of major Northwest cities like Portland and Seattle between May 19th and September 12th that before they commit they need to seriously slow their roll and come back during guaranteed bummer-weather dates like, oh, exactly 4:30 p.m. on

November 21st, 3:22 p.m. on December 17th, 7:40 a.m. on January 8th, any time on March 22nd, and most certainly on June 21st as, despite anomalies, the first day of summer tends to be distinctly unsummer-like, especially when contrasted with weather reports from the rest of the country, where it's basically 72-82°, excluding Alaska, where the government still pays people to live there.

But we're just talking about clouds at the moment. The rain here is a further deterrent, with 152 days a year dedicated to the wet-T-shirt—inspiring stuff. Granted, other cities enjoy the thrill of higher rain totals by volume, whereas in these parts it's all about increased frequency versus girth, ah, versus cubic inches, and the consequently amplified desire to simply give up and put on a solid 15 pounds by gorging on sausage sandwiches, spicy Doritos, and midnight chocolate lava cakes, given that the lack of vitamin D and dopamine create an insatiable desire to feel good, even if for a wistful, fleeting moment, like trying to emblazon that Mediterranean sunset or a robust financial statement on your memory.

The exception to this sage advice ("try it before you buy it") lies within those citizens who enjoy winter sports, particularly mountain sports like skiing, snowboarding, drinking in the lodge, hot tubbing at a friend's sweet chalet, and snowshoeing — or even not necessarily mountain-bound sports but ones that could still technically happen there like hunting and watching football or the new local NHL team, the Seattle Kraken, as much as we thought the Seattle Sockeyes was a much better name given the alliteration.

While the rain dumps depression west of the Cascade Range, it magically transforms those pinnacles and the nooks and crannies in between into powdery-white winter wonderlands — a phenomenon scientists are still trying to understand and Silicon Valley-based venture capital firms consistently trying to monetize with AI and machine learning — with, for example, Washington's Mount Baker ranked #8 on one slightly obscure online survey of best places to ski nationally based on snow volume.

In the interest of igniting some real interstate xenophobia, we'd like to point out that the real advantage of Washington's — and to a much, much lesser degree Oregon's — proclivity for collecting snow at high elevations is the simple fact that most of the competitor states are Utah, Colorado, Idaho, and Wyoming, all of which are documented as having really bad restaurants, including slow service, dirty bathrooms, and a distinct lack of house-made crinkle cut or curly fries, which is tragic.

Speaking of Mount Baker, we're barely old yet-still-got-the-mojo-thank-you-very-much enough to remember the winter/spring/summer of 1998–99, where it literally rained here in the lowlands through July, resulting in martial law and a complete breakdown of the sexual conventions and customs of the local community, leading to desperate, rampant copulation between strangers in cars, waiting for the bus, at Sonics games (they were still here then), and at the original Starbucks store at Pike Place Market. But along with STDs, this weather anomaly did yield 1,140 inches of snowfall at Mount Baker, verified by NOAA as the World Record for Snowfall in a Single Season. Skiers and snowboarders loved it, despite the fact that so much snow basically turned the lifts into rope tows, and the only way to enter the lodge was through the chimney.

The other thing mountains in the Pacific Northwest have going for them is a lower population of creepy, cave-dwelling monsters. Competitor states engage in heavy PR efforts and media-quashing to hide the fact that hundreds if not thousands of ski- and snowboard-bound tourists are eaten each year by Ogres, Chudds, The People under the Stairs, Fairies, Jackalopes, Dryads, and Cave Trolls. Documented fact. In the Pacific Northwest it still happens, but to a much lesser degree.

Those who survive the sporadic attacks here apparently love returning again and again to pay approximately $71.30 plus 8—10% sales tax (Washington; rates vary by how you voted) or $109.00 (Oregon; no sales tax, but they make up for that by employing people to pump your gas, so while in Oregon, as we may have mentioned before, don't you dare get out of your car to pump gas because you're jeopardizing their attempt to recreate '50s-era gas station experiences across the state, minus the racism) for an all-day pass to ride on a lift/gondola/rope tow, complete with jerky stops/unnerving swaying in an air temperature of roughly 24°F, +/- a few degrees based on wind chill or lack thereof, then careen down the mountain screaming "I hate my jobbbbbbbbbbbb" and blasting through as many beginners' lessons as possible without hurting anyone.

Which is a better way to deal with reality than drinking, smoking weed, or rifling through your friend's bathroom looking for old prescriptions.

Skiing and snowboarding are incredibly challenging and physically demanding, mostly thanks to trying to escape the Cave Trolls and such (but remember they're less of a problem here locally), which is why the professionals in this arena work out all the time and are thus so dang hot. To get in top form means putting down the Cuban sandwich — the one called "The Press," with the morsels of roasted pork nestled atop banana peppers, draped with slices of smoked ham and Swiss cheese, slathered with extra virgin olive oil and a garlic tapenade, and melted together in a hot press oh sweet Baby Jesus — and hit the official winter sport training circuit, as outlined below, which we expect you to try after reading this article and consulting your physician and signing a waiver:

- Get some balance, where you stand on one of those half—BOSU ball, half-platform things, then have a friend hit the top of it with a bat. In case you're wondering, the object is to not fall. Or get hit with the bat. Maybe pick a friend with good eyesight and coordination. Yes, this is a real thing.

Okay we're exhausted already, that sounds like enough. But for the record, top-tier snow sport athletes (excluding snowshoe-ers, which is fun but we mean come on they're just walking around looking at stuff then wondering if they should have brought a safety beacon and where their car is) do these:

- Run the stairs (doing bodyweight exercises between floors)
- Do a million "V-ups," where they lie on their backs with knees straight and arms extended overhead, then bring the lower and upper body off the floor by sitting up and touching their toes
- Perform air squats and multi-angle wood chops while standing on a balance board (wood chops are what you think they are)
- Frantically stab-stab-stab-stab! in a 360-degree circle with a training spear while screaming "aaaaaaaaaaaarrgghhhhhhhhhhh" to simulate a multi-pronged, coordinated attack by Ogres, Jackalopes, and Cave Trolls, who've recently decided to form an alliance, at least in Colorado, in an effort to capture and devour more stoned (and thus slow, confused, and easily-netted) skiers, the numbers of which have gone up dramatically since the legalization of cannabis, despite the fact that we said

it's not the healthiest way to deal with
reality but whatever

- Jump straight into the air and tuck their
  knees into their chests while rotating 180
  degrees to land
- Do super slow steps-ups onto a plyometric
  box without pushing from the leg on the
  floor; i.e., the leg up on the box, bent at
  90 degrees, carries all the weight, which
  could be a lot depending on average Cuban
  sandwich consumption rates
- Execute "hero" or "curtsy" lunges on an
  unstable rubber mat where one leg moves
  back, across, and behind, rather than in
  the traditional forward lunge, which they
  just absolutely think is for posers

All of this involves concentrated effort to do
things like maintain a "chest upright" or "your
parents should have taught you this" posture,
track hips, knees, and ankles, work nondominant
appendages (nothing on the human body is symmet-
rical, just saying), develop "proprioception,"
which may be a made-up word, and generally do
plyometric exercises or the repeated, rapid
stretching and contracting of muscles — gener-
ating maximum force in short intervals of time —
to develop power like Kanye and a desire to walk
around without a shirt like an underwear model.
All while breathing "correctly."

It's confusing. Only people with membership in
the shadowy organization known as "allied health
professionals" — whose bizarre behavior is best

exemplified by their hierarchical bureaucracy, complete with weird, coded initials signifying status or specialty, specifically RCEP, DPT, DMD, ACSM-CEP, ATC, and PRC, all of which FBI analysts recently unraveled and linked to the fields of exercise physiology, dentistry, and physical therapy, revealing those professions are part of the overall conspiracy and thus face looming indictment — can help make sense of it.

But be forewarned: Once you get allied health professionals going, it's impossible to make them stop. It's like being trapped in a broken elevator filled with cosplay enthusiasts and one copy of *The Avengers Issue #1* (1963) at Comic-Con. Their eyes literally glaze over, and they become so enraptured discussing their passion they salivate, levitate, and end up chanting what sounds like a mixture of aphorisms and the regurgitation of some highly technical user's manual. What's worse is if this takes place at home — they frequently forget to help with dinner or the laundry, and you'll find them frozen in some pose in the living room, concentrating so intently you'd think they were trying to solve a mathematical equation for landing a spacecraft on Venus.

But it's all worth it. Winter sports offer great workouts in stunning scenery with fresh air and a peaceful, almost meditative ambiance. They also teach grit and how to overcome obstacles, escape from the freneticism of daily digital life, and simply think. Just don't think about work, the price of the tickets, cave-dwelling monsters, or how fast you're going.

Oh, in these parts they also create a reason to look forward to drenching, lowland rain. We know many skiers and snowboarders who actually smile on Sunday morning when the downpours are so heavy we can't see our neighbor's house. For any non-winter-sport folks, the best advice is to book some kind of beach vacation around November 20th, then again sometime around the first week of February. It helps fight off the insanity.

SPORTSBOOKS MAKE YOU AN OVERALL BETTER PERSON

FALL 2021

Washington State recently allowed sports betting to take place at tribal casinos. This is a complex issue that deserves rapt attention and a review of offshore financial accounts hiding assets from both immediate friends and family as well as the federal government, given the former's wont to access piles of bullion to spend lavishly on things that are deserved of owning, and the latter's desire to maintain roads and bridges and political relevance.

Thus the necessity of the international offshore accounting and banking industries, for how else to protect interests in Timbersleds (cross between a dirt bike and a snowmobile), Boston Whalers, secret lakeside cabins, or "work" trips to Viceroy Riviera Maya in Playa del Carmen, Mexico?

Back in March of 2020 — unbelievably in the midst of all the chaos — Washington Governor Jay Inslee signed a bill legalizing sports betting, over several snifters of Remy Martin Louis XIII while chomping on a contrabanded Ramon Allones Superiores LCDH cigar, which brings to mind the somewhat confusing situation of our still-intact trade embargo with Cuba — established by John F. Kennedy in February of 1962 — that, to this day, creates legally confusing situations like the fact that U.S. citizens can legally consume Ramon Allones Superiores LCDH cigars à la Inslee, though it's still illegal to buy or sell them.

Which, as it turns out, is exactly the confusing issue with sports betting in Washington State. Or really anywhere in the United States, given that Washington is only the twenty-first state to legalize gambling on the outcome of any sport, with heavy emphasis on under-celebrated sports like shuffleboard, Rummikub, snooker, disc golf, rock climbing, and any women's professional competitions.

But the overall acceptance of sports betting to include the big ones like football, basketball, golf, and professional cross-country running makes sense, given that for the better part of the last 120 years, tens of millions of patriots across our fertile plains have been just barely, barely restraining themselves from placing wagers on college and professional sports outcomes and heated games of conkers — where one 1900s-era coal soot-covered kid ties a dark brown horse chestnut to a string and his giant-red-and-white-spiraled-lollipop-holding pal in a little AC/DC Angus Young English schoolboy outfit does the same and they take turns trying to break the other's chestnut. By swinging them.

Oh Christ, can you imagine? That was the option. Or possibly working in one of Andrew Carnegie's steel factories. Thank God for TV.

Somehow Inslee and 20 other pro-bedlam-minded governors possessed the wisdom to understand not only that the U.S. citizenry deserved gambling as a reliable source of passive income, but that demand was so intense that if not quelled it was likely to lead to a host of illegal activities — including office wagering, poker nights, dark, smoky parlor room roulette games, and even the possibility of widespread fantasy football leagues conducting "split the pot"-styled schemes, all of which could be made legal by the strokes of a few egos and pens, therefore accept-able to prudish and highly judgmental in-laws of all types. Which we decidedly lack, which we are thankful for.

Thus the birth of Washington's sportsbook indus-try. We decided to see for ourselves what exactly a "sportsbook" is, mostly out of a morbid fear it was an actual ledger or Excel sheet of some kind, where one just sits there and fills out columns and is thus instantaneously bored out of one's mind. But it turns out it's an actual place, typically a dimly lit room with comfortable, tiered, movie theater—styled seating, heat, dim lighting, bad carpet universally patterned in

navy blue, teal, and red geometric shapes,
staffed by a troupe of slightly haggard, desper-
ate-seeming servers ferrying what looks like
every alcoholic drink imaginable to sports enthu-
siasts/data analysts who are undoubtedly in
heaven, given that the two things to look at
besides the white-bloused, black-bolo-tie-wearing
servers (God forbid they're forced to wear an NFL
referee's getup) are digital odds boards and
livestreams of various events.

Oh, you can smoke at a sportsbook too. There are
nonsmoking areas which remain largely vacant, or
at least populated only by minors cutting class,
many of whom must have fake IDs, given that
during our visit it appeared they were drinking
lychee martinis, and who drinks a lychee martini
other than high school sophomores? Also, smokers
have to smoke through a little hole fashioned
into the mask, unless they're savvy and wealthy
enough to purchase Marlboro's brand-new "Down
with COVID/Keep the High DEEPnHALE" flame-retar-
dant red-and-white gas mask thing, the design of
which is based off the ever-popular college
undergraduate   soon-to-drop-out-and-work-for-
Google-anyway "grass mask." Which, if unfamiliar
to you, is worthy of research.

As previously indicated, Washington's sportsbooks
are the exclusive domain of tribal casinos. This
has caused great conflict within the realm of
local rabid NFL fans, armchair quarterbacks,
bandwagon jumpers-on, screen addicts, and stock
brokers (a.k.a. white-collar gamblers), all of
whom think it would just be simply awesome on any

given Sunday morning to pop on over (under the alibi of going to Home Depot) to their favorite neighborhood watering hole featuring a brand-new, sparkling sports-betting sanctuary, what with all the screens and digital displays and hubbub — or even just a steamy ten-by-ten room with a thread-bare armchair, a 12-year-old 36-inch flat-screen TV powered by an HD antenna, and a half-empty bottle of Scotch on the end table.

Alas, it is not to be, for Washington State lawmakers chose a more limited approach than other states that have legalized sports betting, including disallowing Internet or mobile betting options, unlike neighboring and super cool and always-gets-a-ton-of-likes-and-heart-emojis Oregon, where the state lottery earns profits through a smartphone sports betting app as well as tax revenue generated from any Oregonian's sexy Tinder date, as long as things didn't get too clingy and weird.

And there are even more restrictions that will surely inspire steering wheel hand-wringing coupled with screams of "Noooooo" as drivers try and read this article in traffic, which is a bad idea: Washington agreed to leave in-state colle-giate sports betting off the table — as in, no gambling on the outcomes of Washington State public or private colleges and universities. Which begs the question "What's the difference between a college and a university?" which, if you answered, particularly out loud to yourself just now, indicates you may be a dork.

So pay heed: Wagering on games involving local teams such as the UW Huskies or WSU Cougars is prohibited, just like drinking at the park, so please stop. Stop!

There, see? Taken care of, no gambling involving those schools will take place, ever. Nor has it. Ever. Same with the park situation.

It's for the well-being of the unpaid student athletes — particularly the Husky football players, who generate $92 million in annual revenue and $43 million in profit for the athletics program (football revenues fund 85% of a department budget that sustains the 17 other varsity sports and facilities) — while the overall Husky athletics program generates $12.5 million in state and county tax revenue. We want the kids to focus on school and team spirit, not the accidental byproduct of tons of dough.

Besides, these student athletes are high on the hog, what with the recent, generous Name, Image, and Likeness (NIL) grant by the NCAA — which means, if deemed attractive enough by advertisers, any collegiate athlete can profit off their own persona, especially if they make it super brash, loud, and conflict-oriented because the public just loves that stuff (again, as long as the athletes are hot) and will buy toothpaste tube after toothpaste tube (or whatever product needs constant manipulation to appear unique and desirable) as a result.

Oh, Washington sportsbooks also don't allow betting on minor league games, but who cares about the struggles of the minor leaguers, with their passion and commitment and hope, you know? Boring.

And non-tribal card rooms — a.k.a "mini casinos" on Aurora Avenue with hookers in the back parking lot — were left by the wayside and are therefore pressing lawmakers for broader legalization that would allow sportsbooks off reservations, including in privately run neighborhood card rooms (those exist?) and at horse tracks.

We seriously need to locate these privately run neighborhood card rooms.

The new rules do provide for betting on a wide range of sporting events, including other college sports, professional sports, overseas leagues, and Olympic and World Cup competitions. It also allows betting on increasingly popular video game tournaments, commonly called "esports," or…

"Dorkfest"

"The World's Largest Assembly of Virgins in One Convention Center"

"Shut Up, Nerd"

"I'm Sorry, Please Don't Hack My Credit Score"

But now we've wandered slightly off topic. The whole point here is that you can now legally gamble on certain (if not most) sporting events here in Washington, but it's limited to within tribal casinos. Which is fine, because while the state's 29 federally recognized tribes argued that Washingtonians prefer to limit an expansion of gambling and therefore the tribes should be the exclusive, trusted partner (without mentioning their long track record of donating to the campaigns of the Democratic majority in Olympia), they faced massive pushback and lobbying by entities with a stake in the outcome.

In other words, tribes get the gambling because white European settlers took their land, and until there's a better way to make amends, this sounds like the right thing to do.

So pull some cash out of your offshore accounts and hit the casino. No need to drink and gamble in the local park anymore. We hear betting on the over/under on this weekend's Seahawks-Steelers game is the way to go.

BOK! BOK! THE BATTLE FOR SPORTS SUPREMACY ISN'T THE ONLY COMPETITION AT CLIMATE PLEDGE ARENA

FALL 1991

(Just seeing if you're paying attention…FALL 2021)

Shaquille O'Neal is opening what is ostensibly his sixth Big Chicken location inside Seattle's unfortunately named Climate Pledge Arena, working in conjunction with the entertainment ground's executive chef, Molly DeMers. That is, if she is not eaten by Shaq first.

Molly's specific role with Big Chicken's first Seattle location remains a little unclear. Certainly it involves staying out of the way (literally, out of Shaq's physical way, lest she be launched 50 feet across the room by an accidental brush of Shaq's Holstein cow—sized shoulder) and otherwise pretending this is a good idea, given that she emphasizes "sustainability at a large scale" by offering more plant-based food options than any other arena in the country. Which we assume means plant-based simulated meat with appropriate "mouthfeel" (mouthfeel is just a terrible, terrible word) options, since popcorn and pretzels are already plant-based. Well, stadium pretzels actually contain powderized chicken bones and boiled gizzards, but we don't want to spoil this Sunday's *60 Minutes* lead story.

Plant-based meat has come a long way since we tried our first soy patty in college, proffered by a group of dreaded (in both senses) Hacky Sack enthusiasts, who championed its deliciousness despite the fact that it tasted like caramelized asphalt. So Molly sort of backs up our new sports venue's title as "The World's First Zero-Carbon Arena," as does the fact that it was built with "clean" second-century-B.C. technology — specifically elephants attached to elaborate lever systems utilizing giant boulders as counterweights and thousands of Egyptian slaves on rickety wooden scaffolding.

Additionally (when it comes to Molly's locating supplies in an earth-friendly way), all food-related ingredients are sourced within a 300-mile radius and delivered over the course of several weeks by mule trains, which actually only cuts down on undesirable emissions by 50% due to the animals' truly heroic amount of flatulence.

Okay, okay fine, the arena is powered by renewable energy (no fossil fuels are harmed excluding the oil Shaq's stuff is fried in), the builders offset construction-induced emissions by planting forests that will eat the equivalent of all the carbon the construction vehicles spewed out, Storm and Kraken tickets double as free public transit, there are only compost and recycling bins on the concourses, and the hockey ice is basically recycled rainwater from an elaborate cistern which doubles as a dungeon/torture chamber for conservatives, people who think home-less tent encampments in public spaces are dangerous, and any remaining mom-and-pop book-stores, given that Amazon bought the naming rights to the whole place.

But indeed Molly, the former head of the Seattle Aquarium's kitchen — and creator of its somewhat unnerving "Bottomless Fish, 365" fish-and-chips policy — certainly can see the upside to selling fried chicken at her arena, particularly in sand-wich form, to sports fans, given their tendency to express their own competitiveness by tearing apart animal products like big fat lions on the Serengeti, growling and slobbering Nashville hot sauce all over their Kraken jerseys, and even biting any wayward fingers of fellow pride members lacking the necessary agility to deftly and swiftly steal a fry. Or onion ring. Oh man, we bet Climate Pledge makes really good sustain-able onion rings.

Speaking of conflicts of interest, when we think "climate pledge," we certainly think "Shaquille O'Neal," and he's definitely no ham-fisted dummy. He ensures a seamless, loving, and most impor-tantly open (yet somehow lacking the attendant psychological damage) marriage with "the most progressive, responsible, and sustainable arena in the world" — even accepting Molly's plant-based protein stepchildren as his own — with a certain grace he never demonstrated while shooting free throws, as evidenced by the litmus test of all food and beverage enterprises' moral compasses: the menu.

Big Chicken will serve not just crispy chicken sandwiches, but a virtual potpourri of other nutriments, including banana pudding shakes, sliders served "SHAQ'S WAY" (sliders normally have a two-inch diameter; these are 36.75 inches across), salads generously blanketed with fried chicken, sweet potato waffle fries, and boozy shakes. Oh, and sodas — we assume there's soda in there — which we used to call "pop" until someone pointed out how in some regions people say "soda" and in others "pop," so now we're just super confused about what to call it, often awkwardly alternating between the two midsentence, and it's kind of a head trip how stuff like that happens, kind of like how some people call a "couch" a "divan" or think leftover pizza doesn't taste good cold, or how the supposed difference between "dinner" and "supper" depends on time of day when really there is no difference. Right?

It should be noted that anything containing chicken at Big Chicken — which includes the signage, furniture, light fixtures, and employees — consists of NAKED TRUTH® preservative-free, humanely raised, cage-less, hormone-less, and antibiotic-less chicken parts. Okay fine, although it's not called out on the menu, we *assume* Big Chicken only uses chicken breasts as opposed to miscellaneous poultry and/or other creatures' parts, although we're still awaiting evidence of this as our undercover reporter went missing at the Big Chicken Vegas location (since everything "stays in Vegas," we figured this was where we'd find any sensitive corporate documents with incriminating information about how, say, NAKED TRUTH® chicken actually consists of farm-raised, Atlantic salmon…these docs are probably in a vault or something, maybe guarded with lasers). Regardless, we assume he was either eaten by Shaq or maybe is on a hot streak at the craps table.

While it may sound incredibly risky to send a really good-looking undercover reporter with a gambling problem and a host of weird fetishes to Vegas for an assignment, Big Chicken's other locations — Glendale, California; Rochester, New York; and the Carnival Cruise Line/Floating MRSA Factory vessels *Mardi Gras* and *Radiance* — all have restraining orders against Ron (our musta-chioed undercover reporter; we probably shouldn't have divulged his name). Which makes one wonder exactly how much trouble one can get into in Rochester, New York? Glendale, sure, what a festering swamp, but Rochester? Cruise boats we totally get too. People get murdered on those things. Yikes.

Rather than waiting for Ron (who'll probably show up with yet another wife and lots of apologies next spring), we can certainly relay some relevant information obtained via the Freedom of Information Act, a.k.a. Google, about what to get at Shaq's restaurant at Climate Pledge Arena while watching the Kraken and Storm, who hopefully one day will each play their own specific sport on the other's surface, kind of as a combination self-promotion/empathy exercise. Some of Big Chicken's most enticing secretly salmon-based foodstuffs appear to include:

- "Big Aristotle" (real name): Fried chicken breast, Muenster cheese, crispy fried onions, oh my God this sounds so good, sweet & smoky Memphis-by-way-of-a-Scottsdale-industrial-park BBQ sauce, plus the possibility to add bacon
- "Dirty Fries" (also the name of Ron's favorite Vegas-based prostitute): Cheese, bacon, pork belly, banana peppers, and BBQ ranch
- "Shaq Diesel" (in commemoration of his October 26, 1993, hip-hop debut album, which plays on an infinite loop at all Big Chicken locations): An elevated milkshake that comes with Oreo cookies, vanilla ice cream, and whipped cream, which actually doesn't sound very elevated so never mind

In teeny-tiny print on the menu, there's a statement from Shaq's lawyer, Rudy Giuliani, stating, "Consuming the above menu items in this exact sequence literally shaves one year off every restaurant-goer's lifespan, but maybe that's okay since your life is likely pretty boring, unlike mine." Wow, that guy has really lost his marbles.

We do appreciate the voice of this blossoming chicken empire as represented on its website, especially the championing of overconsumption as suggested by various descriptors and calls-to-action for hungry sports fans, including the puns (everyone loves puns; why does everyone love puns?) and phraseology that is at alarming odds with sustainability — which is sort of the theme of this article if you haven't been paying attention — including these:

- "Eat Life To The Fullest"
- "Big flavor. Big food. Big fun."
- "Bok Bok! Big Chicken is serving up some of the best chicken sandwiches with the biggest flavor…"

…oh my God, sorry, we can't stop laughing at that "Bok Bok!" line.

Especially because we're imagining ardent fans of all things progressive, responsible, and sustainable — i.e., the true spirit behind Climate Pledge Arena — reading "Bok Bok!" with a look of stunned, open-mouthed horror upon the realization that, alas, movements based on new ideas, findings, opportunities, and interesting solutions — including those focused on fixing the planet we're breaking, or, as corporations like to call it, "the climate crisis" — require accepting what one otherwise finds abhorrent (or at least at odds with one's belief system, sometimes simply because it's what "the other side" thinks): the economic driver of private enterprise, or, as Shaq likes to call it, Big Capitalism.

Bok Bok! Chop Chop! Gorge Gorge! Cash Cash! Molly must be having a conniption.

Okay fine, our editor is giving us that panicked "cut-cut" across the neck sign with her hand out of fear this is getting too heavy, so we have to stop. The point is, our differences and sharp edges are much more effective at changing the world than homogenization.

What's pretty cool is Big Chicken making use of Amazon's "Just Walk Out, You Will Not Be Accosted by Security, and Please Don't Feel Awkwardly Guilty for Doing Something that Feels like Shoplifting" technology, allowing Kraken and Storm fans to forgo classically long concession lines. Think of this as Amazon Go, but instead of walking out with a bag of pork rinds and a sad packaged salad, you can stroll back to your seat with a piping-hot crispy chicken sandwich and a signature dish, specifically "Lucille's Mac 'n' Cheese — just the way mom made it, but with a crispy Cheez-It® crust" (and a referral to a cardiologist).

All you have to do is (a) have an Amazon account and swear allegiance to it in front of a flag of Jeff Bezos's forehead, (b) scan your "free" Amazon Shopping App to enter — or a credit card linked to your Amazon account — or your palm (not making this up), (c) grab your stuff, and — everyone's favorite part — (d) leave.

The tagline for this Orwellian enterprise is "No Lines, No Check-Outs, No Registers, No Humans," behind which, scrawled in invisible ink, reads, "Please use the palm thing so we can continue to erode any notion that you are anything but a product, and don't watch any more science fiction movies depicting a future of corporate totalitarianism."

Big Chicken, and Shaq himself, are obviously about entertainment and general fun. We like this kind of food, to the point that we have to limit our consumption of it so we don't constantly have to buy larger pants. And we like Shaq; he seems like a genuinely funny guy who'd be super chill and cool to hang out with. So we wish the enterprise the best. Certainly the restaurant adds some lightheartedness to the world's potentially stuffiest, uptight-iest, unfun-iest climate-supporting arena, which, in our opinion, will help people want to make changes that help save our planet, instead of being alienated by a bunch of judgy preaching, of the sort Seattle's "net zero" enthusiasts are wont to do. But it cuts both ways; it will be interesting to see how this place toes the line.

Molly seems pretty cool too. Our sources tell us she's even lobbying to change the sport and entertainment facility's name to something a little more normal.

Enjoy the opening week (next week) — there's lots of cool stuff happening. And tell Shaq we said hi.

ORIGINS OF YOUR OVERLY EMOTIONAL AND LUDICROUS FOOTBALL-WATCHING BEHAVIOR

FALL 2021

Anything can happen. It's not over by a long shot. The Season after the Seahawks Won the Super Bowl began with an away game at San Diego on a super hot Sunday afternoon. Really hot. People were naked in the stands, LEGOLAND melted, and the lions at the San Diego Zoo took over the penguin exhibit's 200,000-gallon pool, complete with lawn chairs and drinks, devouring several of the unfortunate, tuxedoed creatures in the process, more out of habit than hunger, given that it was too hot to eat. It was crazy.

Oh, the game! It was an even match, like most early-season games, as the players hadn't been concussed or had legs torn off yet. We despairingly watched Antonio Gates make a game-sealing, diving touchdown catch to officially hand our reigning Super Bowl champions a big fat 0—1 record.

Of course, despite this setback, that season generated a second, albeit nightmarish, Super Bowl appearance against the New England Patriots, the outcome of which forced a six-month-long, self-imposed media blackout so we could actually function at work. Then the years flew by, with several up-and-down seasons, most of which resulted in playoff appearances and several IRS audits based on our questionable accounting practices, neither of which amounted to much. And here we are today, traumatized Seahawks fans.

Every Seahawks fan likely goes through the same emotional progression during a game, regardless of how drunk they are or how good the team is. It starts with optimism and confidence and nachos, which are quickly replaced by anguish and despair and Tums, followed by a few dashes of hope and adrenaline and something sweet because of all the salt, and concluding with unfounded accusations, coach-like recommendations to anyone unfortunate enough to be within earshot given our complete lack of coaching expertise, and hopefully some bottled water.

Meanwhile, all football fans have the same questions about their team: Why did you run the ball in that situation? Why do we keep getting penalties? Why does the entire team, including the water boys, generate penalties? Are female referees attractive? Why is this so nerve-wracking? Do people think the male referees are attractive? Why do I care? Where's our car?

Fandom is stressful for all of us, with Seahawks fandom being the most stressful in the league. Which may explain why Seahawks fans are some of the most notoriously awful fans NFL-wide, at least on an obnoxiousness scale. Which is better than a felony assault scale, although we all know undercover Seattle Police officers prowl about Lumen Field dressed in visiting team gear to basically entrap the lunatics who are six Bloody Marys, eight beers, and one flask of Jack Daniel's in. Which, frankly, they should. Entrap, that is. The cops. Nobody should have 20 drinks at a football game.

Yet some people, people we want to emulate, seemingly react to stressful situations with a calm nonchalance. There are two reasons why. The first involves having an incredible capacity to handle physical and mental strain à la the Navy SEALs or other Special Forces communities, whose secret maxim that we may have stolen for our website if you read that post works like this:

"Always look cool."

"Always know where you are and what you are doing."

"Even if you don't know where you are or what you are doing, always look cool."

This capacity is a genetic or otherworldly gift (we won't find out until we die), and in the case of Special Forces folks or professional athletes it's perfected through vomit-inducing training, coupled with sharp honing, until it becomes not second but first nature.

The second reason for seeming nonchalance involves being so dense and unthoughtful that the realization of risk, uncertainty, and import is never activated in the synapse, which is also either a genetic or otherworldly gift, the origins of which are revealed upon death. It's best represented by the dolt's maxim:

"Just don't care."

Which is great advice if you don't actually care, but terrible advice if you're a kicker on the 34-yard line with two seconds left and down by two. Or if you're a slightly overweight, Cheeto-munching, pilsner-swilling, middle-aged fan watching that kicker.

Enter Seahawks fandom. Surely many teams in the NFL suffer from season after season of tight-game stress, and we don't realize this because we absolutely don't care about them. But somehow it's different in Seattle, given that even great seasons feature frequent come-from-behind wins, or at a minimum a point differential of seven or less, with the opposing team driving downfield in the waning seconds of the fourth quarter. Or, to reemphasize the obvious, looking at the team and thinking, "Just possess the ball for like three minutes, that's it, just a few possessions oh please." Made worse by enviously, desperately, and longingly watching the ticker of updated scores across the league, some with three to five touchdown margins and three minutes remaining.

Sure, the NFC West is insanely tough, and we as individuals have no credibility, given that we don't like being hit, tackled, wrestled with, or generally touched. The bottom line is, as confusing as it is to watch history repeat itself, and as great as it is that Seattle offers unbelievably entertaining games on any primetime slot (Thursday, Sunday, or Monday night football) — entrancing the fans as well as the networks since networks love the ad revenue pursuant to great ratings from these close games and the ensuing opportunities to buy more gold-plated Gulfstream G650s — this fandom is damaging our mental health.

But why is this so? Unless one is subject to gambling addiction and the associated threats of physical violence from organized crime—affiliated bookmakers, the outcome of a football game is inconsequential. So why do we sweat, shake, pace, fist-shake, feel sick, and ultimately care?

It turns out our messed-up brains are partially messed up by our ability to empathize. Mirror neurons allow us to understand points of view outside our own, the exception being politics, where regardless of the topic or issue the brain goes completely blank and we actually go blind and are literally unable to even remotely want to try to understand each other's point of view, especially if meeting in the middle is required for progress, the benefit of society, or even our own prosperity. But for football, mirror neurons kick in like crazy, as evidenced by the use of the first person plural pronoun "we," as in "All we have to do is not go three and out in twenty-two seconds and…ah, crap!"

These empathetic feelings are intensified while watching football because when we watch our team on the field we are, literally quite naturally, experiencing a portion of the feelings the players have — including what it's like to know that no matter what, we're going home to what is most likely a really sweet pad — because our mirror neurons are at work. Same goes for the cheerleaders; when we concentrate on them we feel lithe, happy, and endlessly encouraging and optimistic about our chances to get a part in a feature film, or at least a modeling contract.

What a disaster, and it gets worse. When the Seahawks win or play well, our noggins release the neurotransmitter dopamine, which regulates our pleasure centers as if we'd stumbled upon a cache of awesome drugs, not that we've done that. Conversely, when the Seahawks commit 972 penalties, thanks to a defense that's so powerful, aggressive, and hungry that it doesn't matter or at least is just the price for being so predator-like, the brain releases cortisol, or the stress hormone. And thus come the pacing and other compensatory measures, like making then gorging upon chili-cheese nachos with pulled pork on top. Yum. But the stress is still there despite this slovenly behavior, in turn lowering our favorite neurotransmitting mood stabilizer serotonin, which can lead to anger and depression, the latter of which is associated with Ecstasy hangovers, or so we hear.

No wonder we're exhausted after yet another down-to-the-wire, half-score-margin Seahawks game, regardless of the outcome. But there's more. We reflect the anxiety the players themselves experience. This includes cognitive and somatic anxiety, or in normal words, racing thoughts in the brain in the face of uncertainty, leading to fun things like profuse sweating and feeling like we might barf all over the place. Which would be bad given the chili-cheese, pulled pork—slathered nachos we just powered down.

And victory is no cure. Another thing that can happen when our team wins, or when we find out that this Friday night our spouse is going out with their friends and our kid is going to a sleepover, is our brains are thrown into an excitatory state thanks to the activation of the hormone adrenaline, which increases heart rates, blood pressures, and desires to watch action movies and drink beer because we have the house to ourselves. Of course, this also happens during the stress and nervousness of a close game, during which the body diverts blood flow to important organs like the brain and heart, but not so much to our stomachs, thus the tummy "butterfly" effect.

If we're worried about our health, or simply don't like the way we feel during a game, doctors recommend taking fandom into perspective and, as with many of the other things we worry about, focusing on how in the greater scheme of our lives the outcome is not that big of a deal. After all (or so these quacks, who probably smoke Marlboros and have questionable medical credentialing, claim), NFL football is meant for entertainment purposes and to take our minds off the stressors and struggles we have in the real world.

Right. Tell that to our bookie. Victory is everything. Here's to the emotional rollercoaster that is Seahawks fandom and, we suppose, the fandom of whichever other stupid NFL teams people follow. We're already prepping nacho toppings for this Sunday's game. We suggest watching a comedy immediately afterwards; maybe revisit *Old School*, *The Hangover*, *The 40-Year-Old Virgin*, or some such quality film we wish we'd written. Just to take the mind off everything and hopefully get a good night's sleep despite the excitement.

FLAG FOOTBALL IS THE SPORTS EQUIVALENT OF KARAOKE

FALL 2021

Adult flag football is a great activity for those still fond of high school thanks to varsity athleticism and popularity, still angry about high school thanks to lack of athletic ability and resultant invisibility, and those shunned in high school or otherwise deemed nerds and dorks thanks mostly to scholarship.

It should be noted the shunned nerds and dorks derive obscene pleasure in rolling up to flag football practice (or any available high school reunion) in 2021 Aston Martin DBS Superleggeras, 2020 Dodge Charger SRT Hellcat Widebodys, or even 2021 Hyundai Velosters, all secondary to fabulous wealth based on actualized options from the purchase or success of their tech start-up that now somehow Disney owns.

Flag football is also a great activity for single people, and people who are technically not single but also not married, so philandering has fewer socio-emotional, mental health, and financial consequences. The latter of which are based on — at least locally — the reality that Washington is a community property state, a fact highly unadvertised by priests and ministers of specific ordainment, or other marriage officiants of vague ordainment through some online course. All of whom, statistics show, are asked less than 2% of the time to verify their legal or not-so-legal capacity to perform matrimonial ceremonies by evidencing proper credentialing, so really they could be phony frauds who just found out about the nuptials online, obtained a believable costume, and are now there for the free food and maybe to bamboozle (ironically) any divorcées in attendance out of the sweet side out of their asset split. Either way, every officiant kind of brushes the details of this Washington State law (which, remember, is what we're talking about) under the rug, given that it means all property, debt, and income of both spouses is presumed to belong in equal shares to said spouses so if things go south, the money gets cut in half, thus the term "asset split." The advertisement of which would devastate the matrimony business.

Flag football is also a great sport for swingers looking for other swinging couples to have swinger sex with. Which likely leads to divorces and asset splits at some point because it simply has to be emotionally unsustainable.

Indeed, flag football is a great way to build community (sexy or nonsexy, depends on the league), get some great exercise, possibly injure an ankle depending on age, realize how hard it is to run a fly route, turn, locate, and actually catch the ball as compared to 20 or 30 years ago, host a "fun" corporate event, or offer an "employee perk" as cool young companies do for recruitment purposes or to otherwise encourage their people to work 65+ hours a week. (A recent perk we discovered during dutiful fact-checking of this article is one local start-up's dedication to "Oyster Fridays," which just sounds like a terrible idea, given that packing an office with folks who've just overeaten raw shellfish coupled with extensive wine and prosecco pairings — the details and specs of which nobody cares about as they just want to get drunk — when the HVAC doesn't work that well and it's an unseasonably warm fall day so the conference room is really quite stuffy likely leads to — at a minimum — disturbing gurgling noises and really weird smells. Or — at a maximum — hallucinations.)

The best time of year for flag football is fall, largely due to the start of the NFL and NCAA Division I (no Division II here, please and thank you) college football seasons and the human male's proclivity to want to be an athletic superstar powerhouse wealthy tyrant. People who orient to anything but the male gender identity have this same propensity, minus the tyranny. Plus it makes sense on a communing-with-nature level; there's the crisp autumn air, foggy mornings, increasingly dark, windblown evenings, the crinkle of leaves underfoot — many with, upon further inspection, gross banana slugs underneath — apple cider with cloves and cinnamon simmering in 40-quart outdoor cookers/stockpots at every corner, squirrels running around in bouts of paranoid schizophrenia harvesting and burying tree nut varietals in various caches — not to mention the camaraderie of the flag football team/league, the bonding, the butt slapping, the sitting there waiting, hoping someone butt-slaps back, then the getting kicked off the team halfway through the first practice because butt slapping is incredibly inappropriate, which is confusing because professional athletes do it all the time, but whatever.

It should be noted that playing modern-day flag football isn't the fun, frolicking, carefree childhood game you knew in the fall of 1984. First, sometimes the quarterback will be some good-looking dude all the girls on the team can't stop staring at. Second, this good-looking dude actually "started" as a Division II college quarterback, and once he overhears all the redundant, disparaging quips ignoring the fact that the Division II classification is a function of the NCAA pairing similar-sized programs in competition for practical reasons rather than an indicator of a player's inherent talent, he'll quickly suggest the disparager line up as a split end — which, upon a quick and furtive Google search, turns out to mean lining up on the weak

side of the formation, whatever that is — and
insist a deep crossing route is in order.
Finally, after his victim flashes amazing 22.4
speed during the panicked, confused crossing
route run amidst gasping breaths, Mr. Division II
throws the ball 35 yards with such velocity and
rotational kinetic energy that it almost peels
the skin off the poor, misunderstood receiver's
hands, then rips the upper torso off the body to
the point one wonders if this is possible, and if
it is, wouldn't the torso have bounced through
the end zone and into the nice lady that lives
next to the park's front yard? Because that guy's
arm is so strong.

Adult flag football is the real deal. Most
leagues feature "gentlemen's," "co-ed," or "ex-
con" formats, the latter of which is certainly
not for the faint of heart. Seasons last six
weeks, games consist of two 20-minute halves, and
professional refs of varying gender identifica-
tion and attractiveness are provided, as are flag
belts, which is secretly a form of bias against
those who own their own flag football belt sets.

Games are never rained out, so there's no
excuse (very prominently worded across all U.S.
leagues, as well as those in Greenland — which
makes sense, people can't live in Greenland and
use weather as an excuse to skip a commitment to
play outside or go visit their in-laws), and in
an effort to support diversity and inclusion
while compensating for the bias against flag
football set owners, every third play must
involve a female player, female players don't

receive extra points for touchdowns, and one foot must be inbounds for a reception to count, regardless of gender (proving more bias, this time favoring males, given that women are much more flexible both physically and emotionally than men).

Another commonality among flag football leagues on a global level is their association with booze, er, "sponsor bars," to the degree that this is listed as the primary or (at a minimum) secondary "member benefit" to joining a league, including "awesome deals for pre- and post-game parties at sponsor bars." Which, upon further investigation, is exactly how the NFL is run, with the bonus of unlimited access to industrial-grade painkillers and anti-inflammatories, as distributed by multinational pharmaceutical companies.

Other member benefits include Halloween parties, Super Bowl parties, local sports franchise viewing parties, "indie" singles/mingle events which also have viewing parties, which is both confusing and creepy, prizes, and, of course, the potential to win a flag football championship.

Naturally, the sport has many health benefits: Studies show that athletes involved in teams sports tend to have better work ethics, organiza-tional skills, and problem-solving abilities. Even more studies show that "attitude follows action," meaning physical activities like catching a prolate spheroid shape (polar axis that is greater that its equatorial diameter,

Lesson One in all football practices) and running for one's life, or running pass routes but not trying too hard to get open because one is terrified of the quarterback, have positive effects on mood and self-esteem.

If that's not enough to convince you to join the team we literally just founded this moment — sign up now for the introductory price of $1683.33 — consider the universal human desire to emulate the admirable. Flag football is the sports equivalent of karaoke, providing the chance to mimic, in public, those whose work we admire, regardless of our own skill, talent, or experience, advice from our peers, or the fact that we should be finishing up that project for work that's deliverable tomorrow but "ah, the hell with it." Supposedly there's also a feeling of identity and community with like-minded people — not to mention competitive euphoria — but we think all that might be largely due to the pre-game party. And pre-practice party. And pre-team meeting party, team Zoom call party, and team cleat-shopping party…

Besides, what else is there to do? Rewatch *Ted Lasso*? Practice is tonight. Just leave that flag belt at home.

YOUTH SOCCER DOESN'T LAST FOREVER AND WE'RE FINE WITH THAT

FALL 2021

Around these parts it's dark and windy and crappy, which means the youth soccer season must be underway. We're talking grade-school level stuff, not high school soccer. High school soccer happens in the fall and spring and possibly a bunch of other times, but it's too hard to pin down a source for confirmation since school administrators don't like nosy reporters prowling about their halls ostensibly to speak with the Athletic Director but secretly looking for organizational drama, scandal, or corruption, which such institutions are ripe with, we suspect.

No, we're talking little kids, in uniforms, running around the pitch in tightly bunched groups as if they're sardines forming a writhing bait ball with which to protect themselves against pods of raiding dolphins. Certainly effective soccer strategy consists of players spreading out for maneuverability and efficient passing, but those four- to ten-year-olds have a really tough time understanding this concept despite promises of pizza parties and candy-based halftime snacks as rewards for compliance because please for the love of all that is holy we are desperate to see you just *create some proper spacing.*

Nope, it's all kick kick, bump bump, the ball rolls three yards, then kick kick, bump bump, stop to tie shoes, do some spontaneous wiggle-dancing, examine own elbow, wonder what the coach and 90% of the parents are yelling about, and other adorable yet maddening and frequently unsanitary behaviors.

But once the little miscreants hit about 11, and especially 12 and 13, we get to witness the joy of ideation and comprehension in action. It should be noted that any phenoms — or those who've enjoyed intense, desperate, specialized, and highly emotional year-round, parent-inspired training — are the exception, and have therefore been drafted — literally drafted — into what are known as Select Leagues. This can happen as early as age six, at which point agents, coaches, and trainers explain to these children that (ironically) their childhood is over so let's go ahead and talk about how moving forward we're looking at this as a profession, complete with strength and endurance regimens, sports psychology, ice baths, access to painkillers — the whole nine yards. People are really putting a lot of faith, hope, and effort into this plan, so slay the demons that will impede your success, little one — namely, friends, family, and religion.

But for the normals, they are just starting to get how the whole game works, which makes it way more interesting to observe. Except for the fact that formerly 20-minute halves are now 30-minute halves, and dang this is still a boring sport to watch, and miserable in this freezing sleet. But at least there's some cohesion, some actual game-play, and some palpable competitive spirit happening, particularly inspired by that one kid's dad, who keeps yelling instructions at his son, even if the dad's helpful framework specifically contradicts what the coach is telling the poor kid to do and the kid is thus yelling back at his dad, "You're telling me one thing, she's telling me another, what am I supposed to DO?" with his arms outstretched and hands splayed in confused anguish.

Welcome to the rest of your life, kid.

Once our intrepid youths outgrow bumper car soccer and start playing like normal people, it's impossible to avoid wanting them to absolutely mercilessly crush their opponents, preferably leveraging proven psychological warfare tactics like fake injuries, schizophrenic yelling, threats, mockery, disparagement, body checks when the ref isn't looking, stepping over a fallen opponent, and all the other terrible behavior we relish in professional athletics.

Unfortunately our New Age children have traded normal competitive conventions for spiritually sound behavior, including earnest effort, mutual support, joyfulness, and generosity, as evidenced by the disturbing trend of kneeling in supportive solidarity after an opponent takes a tumble, crying and grasping various appendages. Then, when little Bobby Joe what's-his-name from The Enemy recovers and limps off the field, they *applaud*.

They must be learning this from YouTube or some-thing. It's utterly confusing, and certainly worthy of some graduate student's sociological or anthropological thesis, research study, or what-ever else ensures them a healthy buffer from having to go work for sociopathic C-suite folks.

Meanwhile, it's common for parents to show an incredible amount of disinterest during the first half of the game. Again, the whole thing just feels like it takes FOREVER, so sure we'll chat up some bystanders in hopes of finding a kid-friendly taproom for a post-match lunch, a place with both the kind of beer we like and food esteemed enough that the rest of the family won't complain. But these conversations can be tough sledding, given that these newfound sideline acquaintances may easily steer the discussion toward their work or their house or their upcoming vacation or whatever other lame thing we totally don't care about because it doesn't involve our forthcoming lunch. Plus it's *Saturday*, man, let's just sit here and forget ourselves, shall we?

But the second half of the match is a different ball game. We're in it to win it yet conflicted, trying to hide our fervent desire for victory and certainly avoid, at all costs, clapping too loudly when we score or yelling slightly mean, slightly encouraging stuff to rub it in like that parent-from-the-other-team does, who is most often a hypercompetitive dad and a total douche.

Like this one time we were losing by about six goals and this well-coiffed dad on the other sideline was all like, "Yeah, Jack, do it again, don't stop, score again." And we were all like, "That guy's a douche and a dork despite his Cotopaxi Fuego hooded down jacket in appropriate fall colors, which is quite sharp and we secretly want." Although his kid was really talented, thus the double hat trick.

Regardless of the outcome of the game, it's important to get the hell out of there as soon as possible to grab that lunch. Don't waste a bunch of time extolling the virtues of resilience (upon a loss) or determination, focus, and teamwork (upon a win) to any offspring within earshot. Frankly, they don't want to hear it. Mostly because they're thinking about tacos too.

If one must stay for whatever annoying reason — coaches are giving post-game encouragement, our kid lost his water bottle, we lost our in-laws — it's vital to lead by example and smile at the other teams' coaches and parents and say super weird yet nonthreatening things like "Nice touch-downs," "You'd be a really good pastry chef," or

"Can I borrow thirty-five dollars?" because that teaches kids how easy it is to confuse people, make them slightly uncomfortable, and perhaps most importantly reference that moment to their friends at a dinner party later, which grants the speaker a form of immortality. Not to mention it's especially satisfying when executed on that well-coiffed dad.

All in all, youth soccer brings joy to many, anguish to few, perspective to the perceptive, and a chance for kids to learn important stuff on their own, including, subconsciously, which parental behaviors not to emulate. The exercise and the teamwork and the learning to compete help them a lot as well, etc., etc., who cares.

Fine. Get on out there and watch some kids' soccer hijinks. Or whatever sport or activity suits their fancy. It doesn't last forever, it's good for everyone involved, plus there's actual knowledge to be gained. And maybe some fun to be had.

See you on the pitch.

THE GENEALOGY OF A THREE-COURSE NFL FEAST

FALL 2021

The best part about Thanksgiving is the cornucopia that will undoubtedly take center stage on the dining room table. This symbol of abundant harvest harkens back to Pilgrim* times, when to express gratitude one was forced to fill an odd-shaped basket with fruits, vegetables, nuts, and flowers. That's right, times are hard, but we're cool with that — after all, check out the size of the cauliflower in this thing, we have it pretty good despite freezing to death.

*Secretly QAnon and the Masons go to great lengths this very day to hide the fact that the percentage chance the Pilgrims placed horn-shaped anything on their dining tables is zero, given that these English settlers thought it was much too suggestive a symbol to place near food, thanks to their morbid fear of wanton lust breaking out, a paranoia spawned from their own unusually high levels of randiness. Plus there was no room at the table as it brimmed with Pilgrim weaponry, including rifles, muskets, pistols, and blunderbusses, all of which gave teeth to the Pilgrims' belief in predestination — kind of like "Yo, we're predestined to deliver God's grace, as evidenced by all the murder weapons God gave us to point in your face."**

**Furthermore, the Wampanoags, the native Americans in this tale, taught these prudish yet conflicted, fashion-forward foreigners (who instinctively knew black-and-white is both timeless and the universal answer to every dressing dilemma, and gigantic stovepipe hats make calves appear more muscular) how to plant corn. So *boom* these pasty-white folks instantly put corn syrup in every food and beverage product possible, inventing two of the marketing world's most sought-after problems to both create and solve: addiction and obesity.

But we're talking about modern Thanksgiving traditions here, not the start of a genocidal rampage, why Critical Race Theory makes people uncomfortable, or how empty calories combined with a lack of portion control makes Americans fat. And nothing screams Thanksgiving more than literally screaming at the television as we watch the annual NFL-sponsored battles between (this year) the Detroit Lions/Chicago Bears, Dallas Cowboys/Las Vegas Raiders, and in the late game Buffalo Bills/New Orleans Saints.

All while ignoring everyone around us to a degree that we get in trouble with our spouse for not helping with the dishes, parenting, or otherwise "being present."

> **Editor's Note:** The Dallas game will likely start late because the Raiders love those Vegas prostitutes so much.

The Turkey Day football tradition began in 1975, when Dallas missed its first-ever Thanksgiving Day game, then again in 1977, when they missed their second-ever Thanksgiving Day game. Wait, what? Oh, in 1975 the NFL Commissioner forced Dallas to surrender hosting duties to the then St. Louis Cardinals because he was mad about being brushed off by several Dallas Cowgirls. But St. Louis proved to be a total drag to watch — both in a competitive sense and a lusting sense, given that their cheerleaders loved barbecue so much it was not uncommon for their uniforms to be splattered with unsightly amounts of the city's iconic, very sweet, slightly acidic, sticky tomato-based sauce, with one cheerleader by the name of Lorena M. Fiddlebots famously gnawing on a rib on the sidelines on live TV.

Which, of course, led to several interstate conversations/battles about who has the best barbecue, whether liquid smoke should be involved, etc., further complicated by detailed explorations of regional differences between the Carolinas (North favors a thin, vinegar-based sauce; South champions a mustard base, with sugar and spices) with even more mind-numbing, intra-Carolina-state variations surfacing based on latitude and longitude — all of which ended up detracting from the NFL's broadcast advertising revenue, so *boom* Dallas resumed regular hosting duties in 1978 and everyone was asked to shut up.

But we're jumping the gun here. Technically speaking, Thanksgiving Day football games (as we know them and not how the rest of the world knows them — because to them it's all about football being soccer, measuring distance and volume through the very confusing metric system,*** and not celebrating Thanksgiving) date back to 1876, shortly after the game was invented.

***Remember when the United States tried to incorporate the metric system via the aptly named Metric Conversion Act of 1975 and people in rural areas — for sure — and maybe in urban areas — hopefully not - actually shot the new speed limit signs? With guns? Leaving ample bullet holes? Message received.

The chronology goes like this: Yale and Princeton played each other on Thanksgiving in 1876, mostly to take a break from talking all the time about how they go to Yale or Princeton. Then a bunch of other institutions followed suit, so truly we have collegiate athletics to thank for this new addiction. Exactly when football became a professional sport is apparently debatable, but basically the first pro Turkey Day game dates to the 1890s.

Real football, however, with those familiar levels of organized violence we've come to expect, began in earnest in the 1920s. The first owner of the Detroit Lions started the tradition of the Thanksgiving Day game in 1934 as a gimmick to drive attendance. He's undoubtedly turning in his grave given their consistent awfulness, current 0—8 record, and newest gimmick to drive attendance: giving away unsold Pontiac Azteks.

A bunch of stuff happened between then and 1966 — including an understandable hiatus between 1941 and 1944 due to the whole World War II thing — with 1966 beginning the tradition of Dallas hosting Thanksgiving Day games. Today rumors fly that Jerry Jones's ancestors demanded hegemony over the event that year or else they'd "eat the world."

The above is only partly true; in 1978 Dallas requested, and received, a game on Thanksgiving Day "forever," after producing legally enforceable contracts signed by every Dallas Cowgirl promising to abstain from barbecue for the duration of their employment.

Since 1978, Thanksgiving games are hosted in Detroit and Dallas every year, with Detroit in the early time slot and Dallas in the late afternoon time slot because they're always hungover.

Previous television network commitments insisted one of these games feature NFC opponents and the other AFC-NFC matchups. Thus, the AFC showcased only one team on Thanksgiving, and the AFC team was always the visitor, which the conference felt a little insecure about and never treated through cognitive therapy, so to this day AFC people don't speak up at league-wide meetings since everyone else is so brazen, loud, and busy establishing their dominance; it's rather intimidating but they (ironically) only do this because they too are insecure.

In 2006, the NFL added a third game on Thanksgiving, played in primetime, in response to the surprising number of families who eat the famous meal at 6:00 p.m. instead of at noon (as heathens do) and thus need something to distract themselves from their immediate families and still be able to drive home. In 2012 NBC began broadcasting this game as part of *Sunday Night Football*, which is great as Al Michaels and Cris Collinsworth are simply lovely, handsome commentators with strong-seeming hands. The league can place any matchup in this relatively new slot — often favoring divisional rivalries to mirror sibling rivalries taking place at millions of dinner tables across the nation — since there are no complicated and headachy conference tie-ins.

Alas, this is because starting in 2014, Thanksgiving games were no longer legally bound to balance matchups between the AFC and NFC or otherwise suffer from weird contractual rules or ties, including those spiked leather bracelets one finds in various adult stores that come with a "safe" word that we forgot so now we're scared. Nay, it's now a free-for-all (the broadcast structure), with games on FOX remaining all-NFC contests and Tucker Carlson rants.

Holy smokes, what a confusing mess. Who knew the genealogy could be so complicated? The point is, Thanksgiving Day is a day to give thanks because there's football to watch, food to eat, people to ignore, and work to take off — except for certain NFL players, turkey farmers, and grocery store personnel.

So buy a cornucopia at the local farmers market, stuff it with some cauliflower, say "you're welcome" despite what the host says when you present it, and get on with gettin' on doing nothing. But be thankful about it. Feel free to start practicing now.